Per
Righteousness

From the ancient Polynesian legends the author traces the history of the Hawaiian people from the beginning of time to the present; documenting their belief in the One Supreme God who created the heavens and the earth; and the first man, Atea, the Kumuhonua. Formed on the sixth day of creation out of the red clay, Atea became a living soul when the Supreme God breathed into his nose. Atea's wife Owa, Keolakuhonua, was created from his rib.

The legends tell of the One Supreme God's ongoing battle for the souls of the Hawaiian people, against Ilioha, the giant moʻo (dragon). From the enticement in the garden to the present time, this moʻo continues to use power, greed and selfishness to turn mankind away from the One Supreme God and His only son, Iesū Kristo.

Painstakingly researched and documented from beginning to end, this is a history book that no one should miss!

"This book is the most important book of our time for Hawai'i. It is critical that we remember God at this crucial crossroad in the history of our beloved islands. We Hawaiians knew the One True God before the bondage of cruel gods fell upon us. We are a spiritual people, and we know that the spiritual affects the physical. Only He, the True God of the Hawaiian people, can convict those who have done wrong of sin, cause them to repent, and to make right. And only the True God of the Hawaiian people can turn anger, bitterness and hurt into forgiveness and healing. Our God confirmed through Hawaiian prophets that Iesū Kristo was His Son. Iesū showed us the way when He, dying on the cross, forgave his tormentors. Our beloved queen, Lili'uokalani said, *'No one is free from his own sin until he has forgiven him who has sinned against him.'* There can be no lōkahi (harmony, balance), for our people or these islands without God, for lōkahi comes from God. We must include our God in the current affairs of our islands, or we will be doomed to failure; for only God is righteous, and the life of our land is perpetuated in righteousness."

Arline Wainaha Ku'uleialoha Brede Eaton

"Mom" Eaton is full-blooded Hawaiian and grew up speaking Hawaiian as a first language. She is a Hawaiian Studies Teacher (Kupuna Program) for the State Department of Education; Protocol Officer for the Royal Order of Kamehameha, Womens' Auxiliary and President of the Pu'uloa Hawaiian Civic Club.

"My kupuna (elders) knew there was only One Creator God, they knew him as 'Io. When the missionaries came, my kupuna listened to what they said carefully. They heard the missionaries speak of the God, Jehovah, from the Bible and knew that the missionaries spoke of the same God. My kupuna realized that the missionaries would not understand this so they kept it within the 'ohana (family). I would hear my kupuna pray to God and say, "'Io, you are Jehovah."

Malia Craver

"Auntie" Malia is full blooded Hawaiian and grew up speaking Hawaiian as a first language. She is one of the most respected living authorities on Hawaiiana. Auntie Malia's mentor was Mary Kawena Pukui, the most respected Hawaiian authority of modern times. Mrs. Pukui tutored Auntie Malia especially in the language of Hawaiian poetry. Mrs. Pukui was the greatest influence in Auntie Malia's life from 1966 until 1983, passing onto her every positive cultural value to the fullest, lest they be lost.

". . . from "Perpetuated In Righteousness" emerges portraits of ourselves, playing integral roles in Hawai'i's history. Daniel bridges the past with today in very delicate terms of God's messages. He presents a number of provocative questions about the ways we see our Creator transmitting different forms of knowledge, and the power of the message(s). Daniel delivers concepts that deal with our current everyday confrontations in our endless search for our Own Truths."

Ben Acma, M.A.
Projects Manager, Bishop Museum
Native Hawaiian Culture and the Arts Program

"As a child of full blooded Hawaiian parents, I often sat in wonder as my father and his closest friends discussed the stories and historical lore of our ancestors that their parents had discussed in their presence during their childhoods. My father claimed our people were directly descended from the earliest tribes mentioned in the Bible. As it was my father saying this, I believed it, but actually could not understand how it could be so. *Perpetuated In Righteousness*, in tracing the Proto-Polynesians' journey to their eventual home in Hawai'i, has placed my father's words into proper perspective.

As my cousin, Henry Opukaha'ia helped to bring Christianity to the Hawaiian people, Daniel Kikawa helps to bring the truth of our peoples' ancestral belief in the One True God, 'Io.

Be not shamed by our supposed pagan heritage as imposed by the followers of Pa'ao, rejoice instead in your true heritage as children of 'Io and His Son, Iesū Kristo."

Ka'ila Williams
Full-blooded Hawaiian, related to Henry Opukaha'ia

"Awesome! Every serious student of Hawaiian History should read this book. The Hawaiian people are truly, *Perpetuated In Righteousness*."

Ed Mills
Bible Teacher, Christian Activities Director
Hawai'i Baptist Academy

In Acts 14:14-18, the Apostle Paul addresses a crowd of Lystrians who wanted to sacrifice to Zeus. Paul asks them: 'Men, why are you doing this? We too are only men, human like you. We are bringing you good news telling you to turn from these worthless things to the living God, who made heaven and earth and sea and everything in them. In the past, he let all nations go their own way. yet he has not left himself without testimony. . . (NIV)'

In this verse, Paul tells us not only the history of the Lystrians, but the history of God's dealings with all peoples. God is never without a witness. There is no one who ever lived who can accuse God of not giving them sufficient information to respond to Him. Believing in this has dramatic influence on how we relate to diverse peoples from diverse cultures. We must approach each person with the knowledge that God has been dealing with them and has given them enough information to render all men "without excuse" (Romans 1:18-20). As different people and cultures are studied, the person with a biblical world view will find that God is already there, working.

This is what Daniel Kikawa has done in *Perpetuated in Righteousness*. In chapters 1-7, Daniel has put forth some very interesting theses about God's involvement in the Polynesian culture. These should excite any serious student of Polynesian and Biblical history to further research. Chapters 8-13 should be read by everyone living in Hawai'i for an accurate picture of Hawaiian history and a clarification of the contributions of the missionaries."

Mark S. Beatty
Th.M., Dallas Theological Seminary
M.A., Linguistics, University of Texas, Arlington
Dean, International College and Graduate School

"The history of Hawai'i nei is like our islands themselves - colorful and beautiful. Daniel Kikawa has incorporated the most beautiful of all Hawaiian history in this one little book. The research he has put into this publication is phenomenal, the number of references impressive. This is *the book* everyone who calls Hawai'i home must read."

Carolyn Winston
Executive Director
Woman's Board of Missions for the Pacific Islands

"Here is a book of lasting interest and profound importance to everyone concerned with Hawaiian history. By carefully using ancient Hawaiian chants and genealogical records as primary sources, the author persuasively demonstrates extremely important theses about ancient Hawaiian history, culture and religion. These powerful theses have tremendous implications for all who are concerned with Hawaiian culture."

Douglas D. Feaver, B.A., M. A., Ph.D.
Dean, College of Humanities and International Studies
University of the Nations
Dr. Feaver is a linguist who teaches Hebrew and Archeology at the University of the Nations. Previously, Dr. Feaver taught at Yale University (4 years) and Lehigh University (30 years).

"Hawai'i is a chosen catalyst for global outreach in the next century. *Perpetuated In Righteousness* is a timely reminder of our rich Christian heritage. You will be fortified to spread the urgent message of Jesus Christ from these precious islands to the World!"

Danny Yamashiro
Evangelist

"Unless we grasp archaic history we will never see the battle between light and darkness among pagan peoples. Daniel Kikawa's history of Polynesian peoples reflects a far deeper understanding, and contributes to a growing literature on world evangelism."

John White, D.Phil. (Oxford)
author and lecturer

"Marvelous! . . . My excitement deepened the further I journeyed into this fascinating book. If only the other peoples had the kind of clear and compelling picture of redemptive destiny that the Hawaiians now possess. . . . This is what we need done for every people group on earth. Daniel Kikawa and the Hawaiians are showing us the way."

John Dawson
International Director, YWAM Urban Missions
Author of *Healing America's Wounds*

Perpetuated in Righteousness

The Journey of the Hawaiian People from Eden (Kalana i Hauola) to the Present Time

Daniel I. Kikawa, B.S., Ph.M.

Fourth Edition

Edited by:
Leon Siu and Tomas Watene Rosser

Foreword by:
Cleighton Kuʻualohaokalaniakea Eaton

Afterwords by:
Pastor Steve Johnson, Daniel Kikawa and Kahu John Kalili

ALOHA KE AKUA Ministries

Perpetuated in Righteousness
Fourth Edition

Library of Congress
Catalog Card Number: 94-72834
ISBN #0964359502

Aloha Ke Akua Publishing
P.O. Box 93
Kāne'ohe, Hawaii 96744

All scripture quotations are taken from the
King James Version of the Bible

Research Assistant - Barbara Afe

Cover Design by Leon Siu

Time line by Dalen Kahiapo

Photos and Drawings courtesy of:
David Kahiapo
Ben Tamura, M.D.
The Bishop Museum

Cover Photo by Peter French

Mahalo Nui Loa to:

Nā Kahu (Pastors)

Ken Kekoa, Paul Kamanu, William Kaina, John Kalili, Duke Aki, Gaymond Apaka, Henry Kahalehili, Rene Godoy, Nathan Hanohano, Gary Holcombe, Steve Kirk, Thomas Kahawai, Etta Lyman, Jeff Soriano, James Texeira, Dean Spencer, Danny Yamashiro, Frank Ortiz, Rick Frasure, Steven Simpson, Vill Galiza, Frank Diehl, Farley Bayudan, Steve Butters, Cal Chinen, Steve Johnson, Les Hokyo, John Frederick, Ron Arnold, Merv Walker, Leroy Metzger, Victor Marciel, Ron Valenciana, Victor Borgia, Clayton Ko Roy Sasaki, Jeff Yamashita and Richard Ing.

The members of Grace Fisheries (Loko Maika'i), Christian Voice of Hawai'i, Island Breeze Ministries, University of the Nations (YWAM), 'Oihana o Ke'opuolani, Ka Ohe Ola Hou, and The Aloha Ke Akua 'Ohana

Charles Scanlon, Kahale Richardson, Uncle Mel Kalahiki, Jan Dill, Mom Eaton, Auntie Malia Craver, Auntie Mary Boyd, Rudy Mitchell, Debbie Lee, Miles Matsumura, Jim Watt, John White, Don Richardson, Ed Mills, Mark Beatty, Chris Cook, Caroline Winston, Cleighton Eaton, Calvin Eaton, Henry Williams, Howard Araki, Dave Hall, Tom Hallas, Barbara Tofte, Fay Williams, John Dawson, Gary Langly, Elanor LeClair, Harry Simmons, Robin Spencer, Tony & Jenny Tam Sing

and the many other pastors, organizations and friends who have prayed for and supported us.

TABLE OF CONTENTS

FOREWORD

When my full-blooded Hawaiian mother was a very young girl, she was *hanai* by her Aunty Ida. Being a personal friend of Queen Emma, Aunty Ida lived in her Summer Palace in Nuʻuanu. It was there that my mother lived and played.

Many years later, my brother and I went to visit Queen Emma's Summer Palace with my mother. The Palace was now a museum. I did not understand my mother's subdued spirit and silence. As we walked the Palace, I could clearly see emotions welling up within her and then being suppressed.

My mother remained like this all the way to our home in Puʻuloa, ʻEwa Beach. There, we talked. She explained that the Palace had been a real part of her life. It had been a rich and alive memory to her. She had played in the garden we had "toured" and played with her dolls under the bed and eaten off the plates that were on display. Now, everything had changed. Instead of a home, it had become a house, only a shell that sheltered things for others to see. Instead of being alive, it had become dead. To the public, it was only, "interesting historical paraphernalia" on display.

This then, best portrays the plight of our Hawaiian people. Our culture once alive, is now dying. Only remembered as a dim memory of a fast fading past.

I believe, in reading this account, many Hawaiians will be shocked by the information they find here, all of which the author has painstakingly footnoted.

As a Hawai'i-born, native-Hawaiian, much of the information written within these pages has been shared to me by my kupuna through: Kukakuka, or talk story time. I have been very fortunate to have many kupuna, including my own Tutu Kāne and Tutu Wahine, impart to me of Hawai'i's past. I have been fortunate to sit at the feet of Dr. Mitchell, Mrs. Curtis, Sir Peter Buck, Aunty 'Io, Aunty Emma, Uncle Harry, Aunty Edith, Tutu Wahine Hao, Aunty Rezentz, Tutu Wahine Mary 'Akiu and Tutu Wahine Maggie Kawena'ole among others.

Through all that these Kupuna have shared, lies a common thread: we are Hawaiian, we are the people of true Aloha.

'Tho' our past has been marred, we once again serve the One True God. The God who we served before Pa'ao's coming. Pa'ao, who was responsible for the introduction of human sacrifice and the perversion that followed. The God "'Iaonalaninuiamaumao", the First (Morning) Star, Eternal One of the (Universe) Heavens.

This then is our true legacy.

E kalamai kākou ka po'e e moku nui. Let us forgive the many nations.

Imua a lanakila e kākou. Let us all move forward to victory.

In conclusion, please read onward. Your souls will be cleansed, a renewing and a refreshing will come. A greater understanding will be given to you, whether you are Hawaiian or you are not.

Cleighton Ku'ualohaokalaniakea Eaton

INTRODUCTION FOR THE CHRISTIAN READER

The One True God Of All People

"The names by which the Supreme Being is called are various and expressive. Almost everywhere they are uttered only with reverence, and that but seldom and not without necessity; in many cases periphrases are substituted, or else gestures. . . The most widely distributed names fall into three groups, denoting respectively fatherhood, creative power and residence in the sky.

The name 'father' is applied to the Supreme Being in every single area of the primitive culture when he is addressed or appealed to.

. . . Among the Koryaks he is 'The One Above' or 'The Master Above', while his Ainu name is 'The Divine Sky-Lord'. . . Among the Yoshua Indians of the American North-West he has a beautiful name, 'The Giver'. the Supreme Being of the primitive Eskimo is 'Sila', whose name reflects excellently the indefiniteness and vastness of the deity of the Arctic primitives for it means, among other things, 'Sky', 'Weather' and 'Power'. The Ainu Supreme Being has three names, all of them beautiful; they are 'Upholder' (of the universe), 'Cradle' (of the child) and 'Inspirer and Protector'.

. . . As regards morality, **the primitive Supreme Being is without exception unalterably righteous. . .**"

> **Wilhelm Schmidt**
> *The Origin and Growth of Religion*
> H. J. Rose, Translation
> author's emphasis

The world renowned anthropologist, Dr. Wilhelm Schmidt, collected twelve volumes of information about the belief in One Supreme Creator God in primitive cultures throughout the world. Contrary to the evolutionary theory, that man's religions began pantheistic (worshiping rocks, trees and the elements of nature) and gradually evolved into monotheistic religions (the belief in one god), the most primitive and remote tribes have retained the most clear traditions of monotheism. They clearly show a belief in **One Benevolent Creator God**.

There is much evidence that even the world's most polytheistic religions **began** with a belief in One Creator God. Dr. Stephen Langdon, of Oxford University, wrote in *Semitic Mythology*, that the earliest Babylonian inscriptions suggest that man's first religion was a belief in One God. He also says that from this belief, **there was a rapid decline into polytheism and idolatry**. Sir Flinders Petrie believed that the original religion of Egypt was monotheistic.[1] Dr. Padinjarekara writes that the ancient Rig Vedas, written between 2000 B.C. and 1200 B.C., reveal much evidence of a belief in One Creator God.[2] The most ancient records of even the Hindu religion, the religion that supposedly has a million gods, reveals evidence of a former belief in One Creator God which very rapidly declined into polytheism.

———————

"This belief both in the moral blamelessness of the Supreme Being as well as His possession of all positive virtues is so widespread and so characteristic in the early cultures that we must say this belief had to be one of the essential elements of the old religion they held in common. . . . The Supreme Being, according to His nature and in all His activity, is not only completely free of all moral evil, he also possesses all of the moral virtues in the highest degree. He is not content merely to be man's model. Immediately after He created man, He took it upon Himself to educate man and teach him how to practice this morality. He reinforces this teaching by threatening and punishing those who do not follow His moral laws, while promising reward to those who willingly follow His commands. He does not abandon the wicked, however, if they repent and try to improve, a point which is made by a number of early groups. Once this life, the time of testing, is over, however, He does not hesitate to reward those who were morally good with a corresponding happy existence and the morally wicked with the kind of punishment which they have coming to them.

In all of this the Supreme Being not only manifests His supreme goodness which leads men to pinnacles of moral purity, strength and bliss, but also reveals His zeal to realize moral justice and beauty. In this way the Supreme Being decorates Himself with new moral virtues."

Wilhelm Schmidt
Ernest Brandewie, translation
Wilhelm Schmidt and the Origin of the Idea of God

Many other religions around the world have also shown strong evidence of beginning with the belief in One Benevolent Creator God, who instituted humane laws of moral conduct, followed by a rapid slide into the belief in many cruel gods who demanded human sacrifice and other inhumane practices. This was true in Polynesia. The Bible clearly shows that God knew of this pattern, Romans 1:18-23 says "*For the wrath of God is revealed from heaven against all ungodliness and unrighteousness of men, who hold the truth in unrighteousness; Because that which may be known of God is manifest in them;* **for God hath shewed it unto them. For the invisible things of him from the creation of the world are clearly seen, being understood by the things that are made, even his eternal power and godhead;** *so that they are without excuse: because that,* **when they knew God, they glorified him not as God,** *neither were thankful; but became vain in their imaginations, and their foolish heart was darkened. Professing themselves to be wise, they became fools,* **And changed the glory of the uncorruptible God into an image made like to corruptible man, and to birds, and fourfooted beasts, and creeping things.**" (author's emphasis)

History, anthropology and archeology have again and again confirmed the truth of the Bible. Many non-Christian anthropologists, who disagree with Biblical scholars about how monotheism began, have had to admit that there is a great amount of evidence that the ancient religions began with, and many primitive religions still contain, a belief in **One Benevolent Creator God**.

This Benevolent Creator God manifested Himself many times as a trinity. Although the Old Testament of the Bible does not specifically say that God was a trinity, the belief that God was plural in nature was clear, and a trinity was strongly alluded to in symbolism. Genesis 1:26 says, "*And God said, Let **us** make man in **our** image, after **our** likeness . . .*" The word used for *God* in this scripture is the plural *Elohim*. Deuteronomy 6:4 says, "*Hear, O Israel: The Lord our God is one Lord.*" This scripture should actually read, "*Yahweh our Elohim (Gods) is one Yahweh.*" The Tabernacle of Moses was made in three parts and the ark of the covenant, upon which the very presence of God rested, contained three sacred items. The Babylonian creation God was a trinity (*Anu, Ea and El*)[3]; *Viracocha*, the ancient creation God of the Incas appeared as three different entities[4]; the ancient creation God of Polynesia, *'Io*, also appeared as a trinity (*Kane, Tane* or *Atea*; *Lono, Ono*, or *Rongo*; and *Ku* or *Tu*). The temple of the Chinese Creation God, *Shang Ti*, was built on a three tiered terrace. There were three gates that led to a three tiered altar which then led to two more sets of three gates which led in turn to a temple with three doors. The Chinese trinity was called Shang Ti, Shen and T'ien[5]

Many Christians and missionaries have a prejudice so deep that they do not realize that it is there. They feel that it is sacrilege to call the great God, *Jehovah*, by any other name. They believe this even though there isn't even the letter "J" in the Hebrew. Many do not realize that this name, *Jehovah*, is a contrived name. It was made by combining the consonants in the name of the Hebrew God, *YHWH* (Yahweh), with the vowels in the word, *Adonay*, to become an impossible *YaHoWah.*[6] This author feels that it is more sacrilegious to say to almighty God, "*I don't like the sound of your name so I am giving you a new one,*" than it is to use the name of the Ancient Benevolent Creator, in the tongue of native peoples. The word *God* is, in the words of Don Richardson, "*European tribal language.*" The word *God* in ancient Europe was used to describe supernatural beings who occupied rocks and trees! The Benevolent Creation God of the Incas, Polynesians, Chinese, American Indians, Australian Aborigines, Africans etc. **never** occupied a mere rock, tree or an idol made by human hands, **he was not created and no idols were ever made of Him**.

Some may say that only the Hebrew name *Yahweh* can be used for God. The ancient Hebrews and even the apostle Paul showed no such prejudice. The name of the One Creator God of the Canaanites was *El*. When Abraham was victorious over his enemies in Genesis 14, a Canaanite Priest named *Melchizedek*, king of Salem, came to meet him. Genesis 14:19-20 says "*And he blessed him (Abraham), and said, Blessed be Abram of the **most high God (El Elyon - El** most high), possessor of heaven and earth: And blessed be the **most high God** (El most high), which hath delivered thine enemies into thy hand. And he (Abraham) gave him tithes of* *all.*" Abraham did not say, "*Just wait a minute, you heathen priest! Don't you dare bless me in the name of your heathen god and claim that my victory was caused by your heathen god, El!*" Abraham instead acknowledged Melchizedek and his God, El, by giving the first recorded tithe to him! Is it also sacrilegious when the Bible says that Jesus is a priest forever after the order of Melchizedek, that heathen Canaanite, and of his heathen God, El (Hebrews 7)?

The word for God, *Elohim*, mentioned earlier, is the plural form of *El*. God Himself confirmed that He was El, Exodus 6:2-3 says, "And God (Elohim) spake unto Moses, and said unto him, I am the *Lord* (YHWH): And I appeared unto Abraham, unto Isaac, and unto Jacob by the name of *God Almighty* (*El Shaddai* - El Almighty), but by my name Jehovah (YHWH) was I not known to them." This scripture says that Abraham, Isaac, and Jacob knew God by the name El. The Hebrew name *Elijah* means *El is Yahweh*. El and his various names were incorporated into the Hebrew language as it was being formed (Abraham spoke Chaldee. Hebrew was formed some time after 1400 B.C.[7]). It is found in the Hebrew words *Elohim* (El plural), *El Elyon* (El most high), *El Roi* (El who sees me), *El Shaddai* (El Almighty), etc. and in names like *Elijah* (El is Yahweh), *Michael* (Who is like El?), *Gabriel* (Man of El), and the author's good Jewish name, *Daniel* (My Judge is El).

Who was this God, El? El was the highest God in the Canaanite pantheon. The *Theological Wordbook of the Old Testament* says that "The name 'El' is a very ancient Semitic term. It is also the most widely distributed name among Semitic-speaking peoples for the deity, occurring in some form in every Semitic language except Ethiopic. . . the term El was used in reference to **a personal god and not merely as a generic term** in the ancient Semitic world."[8] (emphasis-the author's) In *Ugarit*, he was the father of gods, men and the *'creator of creatures'*. El was also the *'creator of the earth'* of the Hittites and Phoenicians and one of the Babylonian trinity. He was wise and kind, showing sadness and happiness, but not anger.

However, the knowledge of El, like the creation God of Babylon, experienced much corruption. El was said in some texts to have created other gods by procreation. One text even describes El copulating with two women in order to procreate the gods Shahar and Shalem and then a series of other gods![9] Because the knowledge of El was corrupted, should we now throw words like Elohim, El Shaddai, Daniel and Michael out of the Bible? Should we throw YHWH (Yahweh, Jehovah) out of the Bible because He said himself that He was El? Should we throw YHWH out of the Bible because, at one time, YHWH worship was corrupted to the point that the Hebrews worshipped Yahweh, Baal, Tammuz, Ashtoreth, Molech and other gods at the same time? (2 Kings 17:16-17, 1 Kings 11:5-7, Ezekiel 8:14) In fact, the Hebrews, at one time, worshipped a pantheon of gods in the very temple of YHWH. (2 Kings 23:4)

It is time that Christians reclaimed the many beautiful names of the One Creator God in native languages instead of falling into Satan's trap and destroying them. We should reclaim those names and wash the dung of corruption off of them instead of giving them up to Satan. We must cast off the corruption that Satan has thrown on the many beautiful names of God in native languages.

God is the creator of all nations, tongues and peoples and is spoken of in each language. The Hawaiian people and others like the Navajo did not reveal the knowledge of their Supreme Benevolent Creator God to the white man because their God was too precious to them. They could not stand to see their beloved Creator belittled, ridiculed, laughed at, and called the devil by the white man.[10]

Instead of destroying and ridiculing the native names of the Creator God, we should help preserve them as a legacy for these peoples. It is their legacy of God's enduring interest, involvement and care for their culture and people! Christians should cease representing Jesus as the Son of the foreign God of a foreign people, especially if these foreigners had never shown concern for nor had any involvement in the lives or culture of the natives. We should instead introduce Jesus as the Son of **their creator God**. God lovingly created them from the beginning, never left them without a witness and, in his great love for them, even sent His only begotten Son, Jesus, to die for them!

Don Richardson was a missionary to a tribe of primitive people in Irian Jaya. These people were head hunting cannibals who held treachery as their highest virtue. When Don tried to tell them the story of Jesus, they thought Judas was the hero! I believe that the Lord had placed Don with one of the most vicious and horrible tribes on earth for a very important reason. Don found that, even in a tribe like this, God did not did not desert these people and leave them without a witness of Him. He found several very beautiful examples of God's love and plan of salvation in the culture and traditions of this tribe.

The book Don wrote about his experiences, *The Peace Child*, has become a best seller. The Lord loved these and other native peoples so much that he used Don to change our thinking about them. God wants to change our thinking so that we will not approach native peoples with a condescending pride but with a humble awe. We should be in awe that God would use foolish and imperfect people like us to share the wondrous message of His Son with His dearly beloved native peoples. We should humbly and eagerly look for the beautiful witness God has left in the cultures of His beloved native children. What unique gifts did God leave for them which will give fullness, beauty and insight to the rest of His children? How arrogant we are to think that God would have forgotten them! Many missionary efforts have ended in miserable failure because of unconscious cultural prejudice and insensitivity. This should not continue to happen. Let's see how the Lord, long ago, used the Apostle Paul as an example for us.

Paul was so strict and narrow minded in his Jewish tradition that he could not see in the Holy Scriptures that Jesus was the Messiah. He thought that Jesus was the heretics' heretic for calling himself the Son of his God. In his indignation and self-righteous anger, he brought the deaths of many Christians. Paul felt that he was doing a great service for his God. He was on his way to do more harm to Christians when God had to finally knock him flat on his back, blind him and speak to him in an audible voice. Then Paul finally understood that Jesus was God.

After this experience, Paul realized how narrow minded he had been. His changed and humbled nature made him the perfect Apostle to the Gentiles (non-Jewish peoples)! God appointed him as such in Acts 9:15. Paul also became so open minded that he said he was free and no longer under Jewish law. (Galatians 5:18). Paul no longer followed the traditions of men but believed he should become "*all things to all men*" that he "*might by all means save some.*"(1 Corinthians 9:22) As long as Paul was guided by the Holy Spirit (who revealed the Holy Scriptures to him in a new way) and by the love of his fellow man, Paul felt that he was free to do all things. Therefore, he lived like the Gentiles among the Gentiles and accepted their customs so that they would be more open to him when he told them about the Gospel. He even rebuked Peter because Peter held Jewish prejudices against the Gentile Christians! (Galatians 2:11-14) His open-mindedness was very evident in the way he handled the Athenians.

The Athenians had hundreds of gods. Acts 17:16 says that Paul was distressed by all the idols that were there. On Mars Hill, where Paul addressed the Athenians, there were hundreds of idols, yet Paul picked a monument among all of these heathen idols and told the Athenians that he would tell them about the "Unknown God" it represented. (Acts 17:23) Paul then proceeded to say, "*God that made the world and all things therein, seeing that he is Lord of heaven and earth, dwelleth not in temples made with hands; Neither is worshipped with men's hands, as though he needed any thing, seeing he giveth to all life, and breath, and all things; And hath made of one blood all nations of men for to dwell on all the face of the earth, and hath determined the times before appointed, and the bounds of their habitation. That they should seek the Lord, if haply they might feel after him, and find him, though he be not far from every one of us:*" Paul then proceeded to quote a poem written by *Aratus* whose poem, *Phaenomena*, was the most popular and famous poem in Greece after Homer's Iliad and Odyssey.[11] He said, "***For in him we live, and move, and have our being; as certain also of your own poets have said, For we are also his offspring.*** *Then Paul concludes, "forasmuch then as we are the offspring of God, we ought not to think that the Godhead is like unto gold, or silver, or stone, graven by art and man's device."* This poem by Aratus which Paul used attributes what he quoted to Zeus! This poem also speaks of all the signs of the Zodiac! The Encyclopedia Britannica says, "*The opening invocation to Zeus has become famous because it was quoted by Saint Paul.*"[12] This same Zeus saw women he desired and had sex with them. He also displayed all of the negative human emotions! Yet Paul used this poem without fear in order to find common ground to relate to the Athenians. As quoted earlier, Paul said, "*That they should seek the Lord, if haply they might feel after him, and find him, though he be not far from every one of us:*" (The author would like caution here, however, about using the name of a creator god **with no clear evidence that this god was benevolent before corruption. Research is of supreme importance because, many times, Satan poses as the creator god of all.**)

For what Paul did, many modern Christian Sauls and pharisees would have crucified him! Modern pharisees, in their "Christian" traditions, pride and prejudices, have in effect said to native peoples they were attempting to "evangelize", "*Oh, you poor, foolish and immature heathen believing in so many gods! You should follow us Christians who have the lofty and superior knowledge of the Only Supreme Creator. You must throw away all of your ridiculous, filthy heathen idols and all of your filthy heathen culture and adopt our culture and*

*worship our God in our way which is so superior to yours and
which, therefore, naturally pleases God."* No wonder
missionaries with this approach have not been effective and
have caused much harm to the Gospel. Harsh and prejudiced
missionaries' rejection of native cultures as evil and containing
no redeemable qualities is one of the main reasons for the
rejection of the Gospel by many Hawaiians and other native
peoples today.

　　　The Korean Church is a good modern example of the
effect of these two diverse methods of evangelism. The
Catholics arrived in Korea first and preached in the name of
their "foreign" God. They received very little response. In
1884, Protestant missionaries, after researching the Korean
Supreme Being, began using the name of the benevolent
Creator God, *Hananim,* in their preaching. They taught that
Jesus Christ was the Son of Hananim and that Hananim had
sent Jesus to bring the Koreans into a new relationship with
Himself. Thousands of Koreans listened in awe, these
missionaries knew so much about their God, Hananim! The
news began to shake Korea.[13]

　　　This is one of the reasons a great revival started in
Korea. As we can see today, the fruit of this revival is long
lasting. Korea now sends out more missionaries than any other
country in the world and the three largest churches in the
world are in Korea. What a tremendous difference using the
name of Hananim has made for the Gospel of Jesus Christ in
Korea!

　　　Let us, as Christians, humble ourselves and repent of
our sins of cultural prejudice which have hurt native peoples
and damaged the work of the Gospel in native lands. Let us
reintroduce to native peoples the **One True God of all people**

who lovingly created them in His image and, because of His great love for them, sent His Son, Jesus, to reconcile them to Himself.

E Komo Mai

Come

PROLOGUE

It is time again for our true story to be told. Our story that was hidden and cast down for many ages. It is time for all peoples to understand from our story that a mighty battle rages for the souls of men, between *Ilioha*, that great serpent and *'Io*, the One True God. The great spiritual battle that rages even now for our beloved islands and our people.

Bear witness to the story. . .

A heaving, treacherous sea, like the rise and fall of a giant's chest breathing deeply . . . black against the blinding sky. Above the pounding waves and howling winds could be heard the chilling cries of children as their mothers and elders struggled to calm their fears. Mingled with these cries were the sounds of screeching pigs and whimpering dogs. Women, children and beasts huddled together desperately beneath a canopy of woven grass, tree bark, and sticks, upon a platform joining two wooden hulls: the voyaging canoe.

Upon these hulls our *kupuna* (ancestors) fought valiantly in the perils of the storm, holding steady in the powerful grip of the swells and currents. Prayers were fervent during these moments which turned into endless days. If one dared, one could hear the priest chanting words of faith, the sacred words of 'Io, "*Move on, O Whakatau, move on to Hawaiki, establish there thy house, as though it were under the sacred care of 'Io.*" (ancient chant of the Ngati Hao Maori)

Though tossed amidst the sometimes merciless Pacific Ocean, our ancient mariners knew the ways of the wind, waves, stars and birds – Wayfinding. It was an understanding of nature that is deeply ingrained in our culture. It was the mysteries of 'Io making wise their simple but trusting hearts. For they were following the ancient prophecy of the Star of Gladness which they called Hōkūle'a. They knew that after the storms relented, *Akua* would bend a rainbow in the heavens and use rays of light as arrows to break forth in the light of dawn, an island in the midst of the sea.

In the still of calm waters and quiet eves, our kupuna would gaze deeply into the starlit skies and were awed by the presence of the Almighty. His beacons of light would guide their ocean paths and His breath would fill their sails as their hulls gracefully skimmed the liquid space beneath.

Hungry and weather-beaten, but full of faith, they journeyed on until at last, from the far horizon, the Hawaiian islands were birthed from the sea! It was an expression of 'Io's love waiting patiently to welcome our wearied seafarers of old. Mighty 'Io the Creator of All Things. 'Io the Eternal, who ever was, is now, and ever shall be.

In the Beginning . . .

" *'Io dwelt within the breathing space of immensity. The universe was in darkness, with water everywhere. There was no glimmer of dawn, no clearness, no light. And He began by saying these words, that He might cease being inactive, 'Darkness become a light possessing darkness.' And at once light appeared.*"

" *'Io then looked to the waters which compassed Him about and spake a fourth time saying 'ye waters of Taikama, be ye separate. Heaven be formed.' Then the sky became suspended. 'Bring forth thou Tupuhoronuku.' and at once the moving earth lay stretched abroad.*" (ancient chant of the Ngati Kahungunu Maori)

At the dawn of creation was an eternal void. Emptiness and blackness that cannot be fathomed by fragile human minds. Then, light streamed forth from the corridors of eternity. The land, sea and sky appeared. The moon and stars were set to shine in darkness. Nature's song could be heard filling all the earth; 'twas the language of beast and fowl. Yet the land, freely roamed, was void. Neither creature nor beauty could satisfy the longing of He who spoke all things into existence.

Thus was *Atea*, the *Kumu Honua*, fashioned from the red clay and *Iwi, Ke Ola Ku Honua* formed from his rib. Creator and creation communed peacefully in the soft brilliance of the 'aina (the land). Atea and Iwi had much aloha for their *Akua Most High*.

However, at a distance, one who lay hidden in an 'ōhi'a tree would forever change the course of all peoples. His presence seemed out of place in *Kalana i Hauola*. He moved with cunning and was wise – *Ilioha*, the *Mo'opeloa*, the Great Serpent. Ilioha was filled with a blinding desire to be worshipped and adored by Atea and Iwi as 'Io was. He entangled Iwi in a web of lies and Iwi was tricked into eating from the forbidden *'Ōhi'a Hemolele*. Atea also ate even though 'Io had warned them that eating of this forbidden *'Ōhi'a* Hemolele would bring a terrible curse upon the earth; a curse that would bring great sorrow and hardship upon all mankind. Atea and Iwi were driven by 'Io out of Kalana i Hauola; this was the beginning of many sorrows. Still, 'Io's aloha went beyond the *hala* (sin) of our first kupunas. 'Io commanded that the silent stars proclaim to all peoples yet unborn, the coming of a Deliverer who would free the *honua* (earth) from the curse.

Generations later there arose a descendant of Atea named *Nu'u*, whom 'Io entrusted to build *Te Tai Toko*, a large canoe that would hold two creatures of every kind. Because of the great evil of man on the face of the earth, water would flood the honua and everything that breathed would die. Only Nu'u and his *'ohana* (family) were saved from the great flood that rose above the mountains.

Days upon days and night after endless night passed; finally the waters subsided. Nu'u and his 'ohana were awed by the beautiful colors that stretched across the sky, 'Io's rainbow. *'A 'ole lawe wai* (No more flood.) 'Io longed for peace to rule in the hearts of Nu'u's 'ohana and their *mo'opuna* (descendants), but their aloha for Him would have to be strong.

Beyond many setting suns and rising moons, a man named *Nimrod,* with his charismatic personality and cunning speech, convinced the children of Nuʻu to build a magnificent tower to study the stars. This was the mark of Ilioha, the father of lies, for the stars declared the message of the coming Messiah; they were not made for the exaltation of man through fortune telling and occultic practices. ʻIo destroyed this tower, scattering and confusing the *ʻōlelo* (speech) of the people to save them from themselves.

Our Polynesian genealogies also speak of our journey from *Uru*, called Ur by our Chaldean brothers. Our Kupuna sailed from the Persian Gulf down to the Arabian Sea and on to *Irihia* (India), where our people lived for many years. The long voyage had begun! Our ancestors could not contain the desire bursting from their spirits! It was ʻIo calling them saying, "*To the East, in the midst of the great ocean — follow the rising sun!*" So the course was set to the rising sun, ʻIo's creation of light and life. The west beyond which lay *Po*, the great darkness and death, was left in the canoe's wake. Above all, the stars of ʻIo guided them, and after every storm, his rainbow graced the skies. "*Follow the rising sun,*" their hearts echoed. It became a song of faith which led them onward.

Our ancestors sailed on through many lands: Burma, Sumatra, Java, leaving some of our number behind. But ʻIo and the rising sun continued to call us onward. We spent some time in the islands of New Guinea and Fiji with our dark brothers before moving on to our greatest feat of all . . . the conquest of the Great Ocean.

Islands were raised, or (in the navigators' colorful language) fished out of the sea. *Tonga, Samoa, Aitutaki, Ra'iatea, Huahine, Tuamotu, Nuku Hivva, Hiva Oa* and *Tahiti* were fished from the great sea. The many islands of central Polynesia were discovered and inhabited.

Guided by the ancient prophecy of the star Hōkūleʻa, shining brightly in the northern sky, our ancestors turned north and plunged into the unknown. They believed that steering towards this star in the constellation of *Boötes* (the coming Shepherd-Judge) would bring landfall beyond the dark ocean. The stars spoke of Boötes reaching for His Crown, the *Corona Borealis*, with His right hand and holding a sword with his left hand, ready to slay Moʻopeloa, the great serpent, who is trying to steal the crown. The hearts of our kupuna leaped with great joy at the sight of Hōkūleʻa, for this star revealed ʻIoʻs final victory and judgement over Ilioha. The curse, the sorrows and hardships of sin, would one day be broken!

A great leap of faith was required to continue on into thousands of miles of empty blue on blue. In the northerly direction of this wonderful star, our ancestors searched for and found our new home. We had finally found the place ʻIo had provided for us! Here we worshipped ʻIo, in this land so much like Atea's first home.

ʻIo has made from one blood, all nations of people to inhabit the face of the earth. It is inherent in our being to yearn for Him, to seek and find Him, because in Him we live and move and have our being. All cultures are His offspring. Polynesia is the bounds of our dwelling as Polynesians; in it we honored and worshipped the Most Excellent Supreme with the talents and knowledge He had given to us.

However, the darkness rages to overcome the Light. Under many new names - *Kanaloa, Tangaroa, Miru, and Whiru,* the Prince of Darkness once again approached us to steal us away from the ways of ʻIo. As his darkness swept in from *Po* in the west, he nearly succeeded in destroying all knowledge of our True God, 'Io, in the Western and Central Pacific. He bore in his dark wings war, human sacrifice and the oppression of the poor. In the North (Hawai'i), his servant, the priest *Pa'ao*, sailed in from Tahiti and built the first *luakini* (human sacrifice) *heiau* (temple) in Hawai'i. He killed the priests of 'Io and, as it was done before at the great tower, corrupted the knowledge of 'Io and His chants of creation. The bondage created by Pa'ao's new religion took a terrible toll on our people, especially the *maka'āinana* (common people). Terrible wars also swept through our islands as the great serpent enticed the ali'i (chiefs) to pride and greed.

However the flames of eternity burned in the hearts of the surviving priests of 'Io who set sail in their canoes from Hawai'i to preserve the worship of the One True God. And yes, a few brave souls remained who would not be corrupted by Pa'ao, to preserve the knowledge of 'Io for the sake of future generations. These were forced to hide the ways of their Mighty Akua in humble silence.

In Kohala a child, who would be known as the *Lonely One,* was born. This fearless young chief, *Kamehameha,* was the instrument of the all powerful 'Io to unite the chiefs and set the stage for the coming of His Son, *Iesū Kristo* (Jesus Christ).

On October 3, 1819, five months after the death of Kamehameha, the evil system of Pa'ao was broken by our ancestors. The heiaus were desecrated and the idols destroyed. Our Akua Most High, whom we had worshipped long before the coming of Pa'ao, was preparing the way for His return.

In March of 1820, the servants of our One True God, the missionaries, arrived. They brought the Good News of

Jehovah (the name of 'Io in the western world) to Hawai'i. 'Io had used a young Hawaiian named Henry *Opukaha'ia* to inspire these missionaries to surrender their lives for our people. Although chosen to be a priest of the religion of Pa'ao, Henry became an inspiration to all, after he met his savior, Iesū Kristo.

The lives of the missionaries, though far from perfect, became a light shining in the darkness of Polynesia. Their light was the message of the death and resurrection of 'Io's Son, the promised Deliverer, Iesū Kristo, who would free the Hawaiian soul. A time of peace and prosperity was ushered in for us, especially for the common people. Our nation became one of the greatest nations on earth in the ways of 'Io; a beacon of spiritual light and life to other peoples of the Pacific.

However, the serpent, that most deceptive of creatures, again prevailed. He deceived some of our *ali'i* (chiefs) and some of the children of the missionaries to accept the temptation of his spirit of greed, pride and lust for power. The people began to slip away from the ways of 'Io. This same spirit was the root which caused the overthrow of our beloved Queen *Lili'uokalani*, a servant of Iesū Kristo, and the loss of our *'āina* (lands). This same spirit continues to reign over these islands today. The loss of our lands has also caused many maka'āinana (common people) to stumble into Ilioha's trap of bitterness.

Kulikuli! Noho Mālie. (Hush! Sit quiet.) Listen with your heart to a people crying; souls wailing in a darkened Polynesia. They are a people grappling for an identity, a heritage overshadowed and lost by the passing of time. Deliver us, O 'Io, our One True God. Heal our *'āina* and let not the aloha you placed in our hearts turn to hatred and bitterness!

Give us victory in the spiritual battle that rages even now for our beloved islands and our people.

We live in a critical moment in time. Will our land and our people be a beacon of righteousness, aloha and peace as never before, or will our 'āina, our land, and our people be destroyed?

Ha'ina 'ia mai ana ka puana
(Let the echo of our song be heard)

UA MAU KE EA O KA 'ĀINA I KA PONO
The Life of the Land is Perpetuated in Righteousness

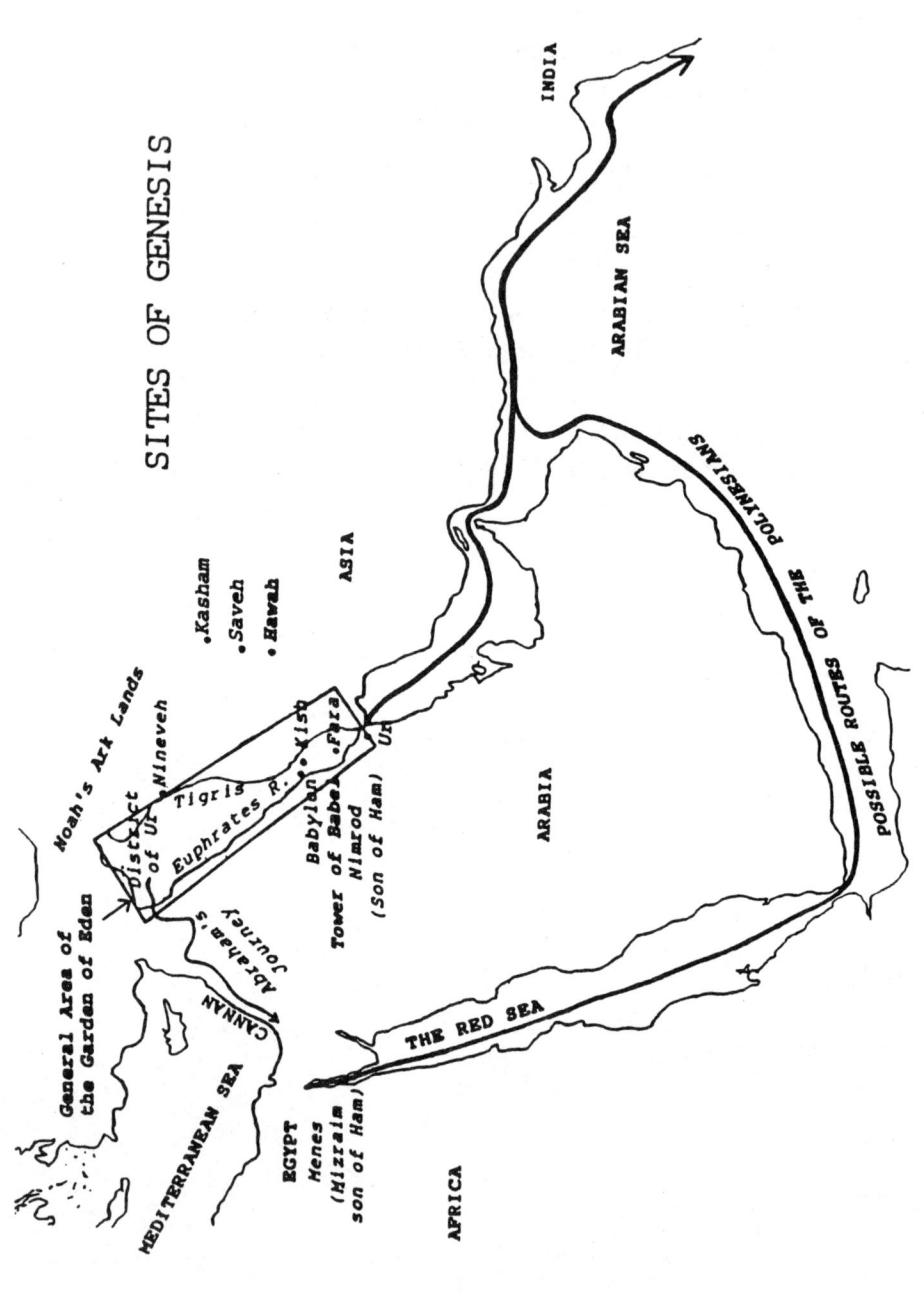

SITES OF GENESIS

General Area of
the Garden of Eden

Noah's Ark Lands

District
of Ur · Nineveh

·Kasham
·Saveh
· Havah

Tigris

Euphrates R.

Babylon · Kish
·Fara
Tower of Babel
Nimrod
(Son of Ham)

Ur

ASIA

ARABIA

INDIA

ARABIAN SEA

POSSIBLE ROUTES OF THE
POLYNESIANS

Abraham's
Journey

CANAAN

MEDITERRANEAN SEA

EGYPT
Menes
(Mizraim
son of Ham)

THE RED SEA

AFRICA

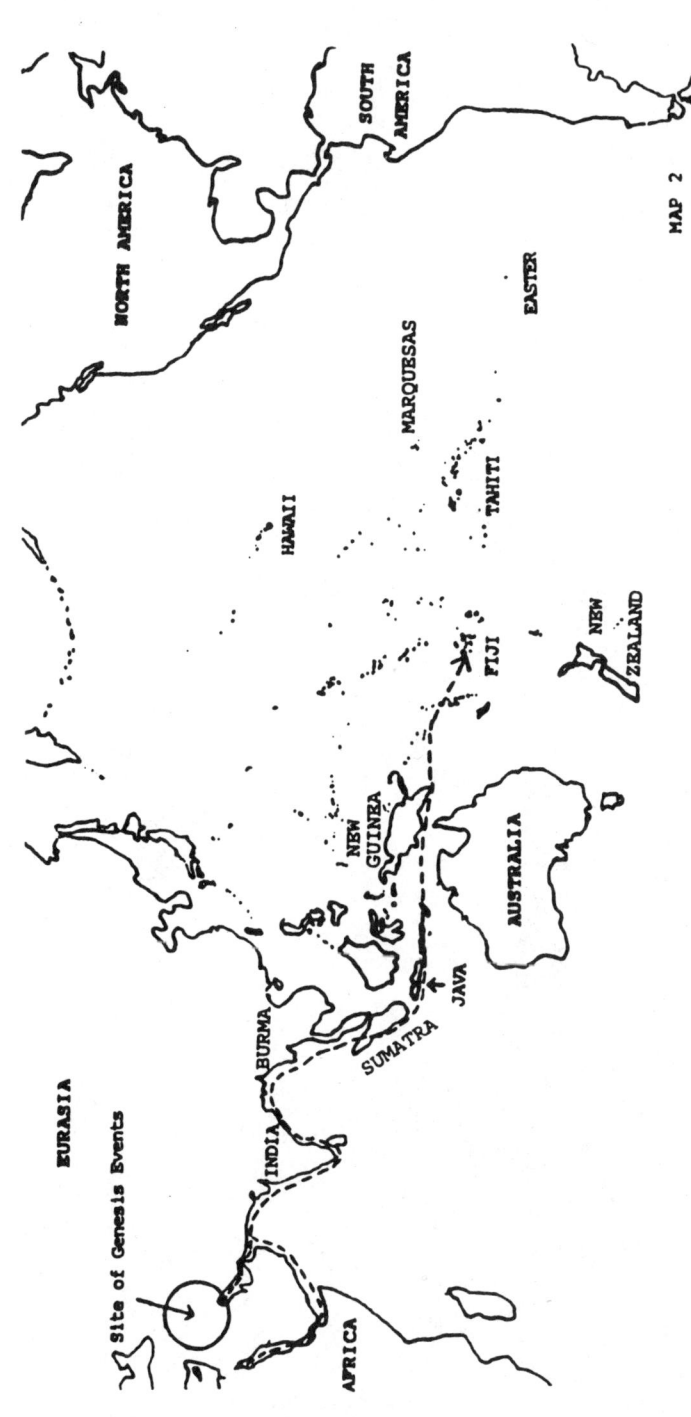

PROBABLE ROUTE OF THE POLYNESIANS

MAP 2

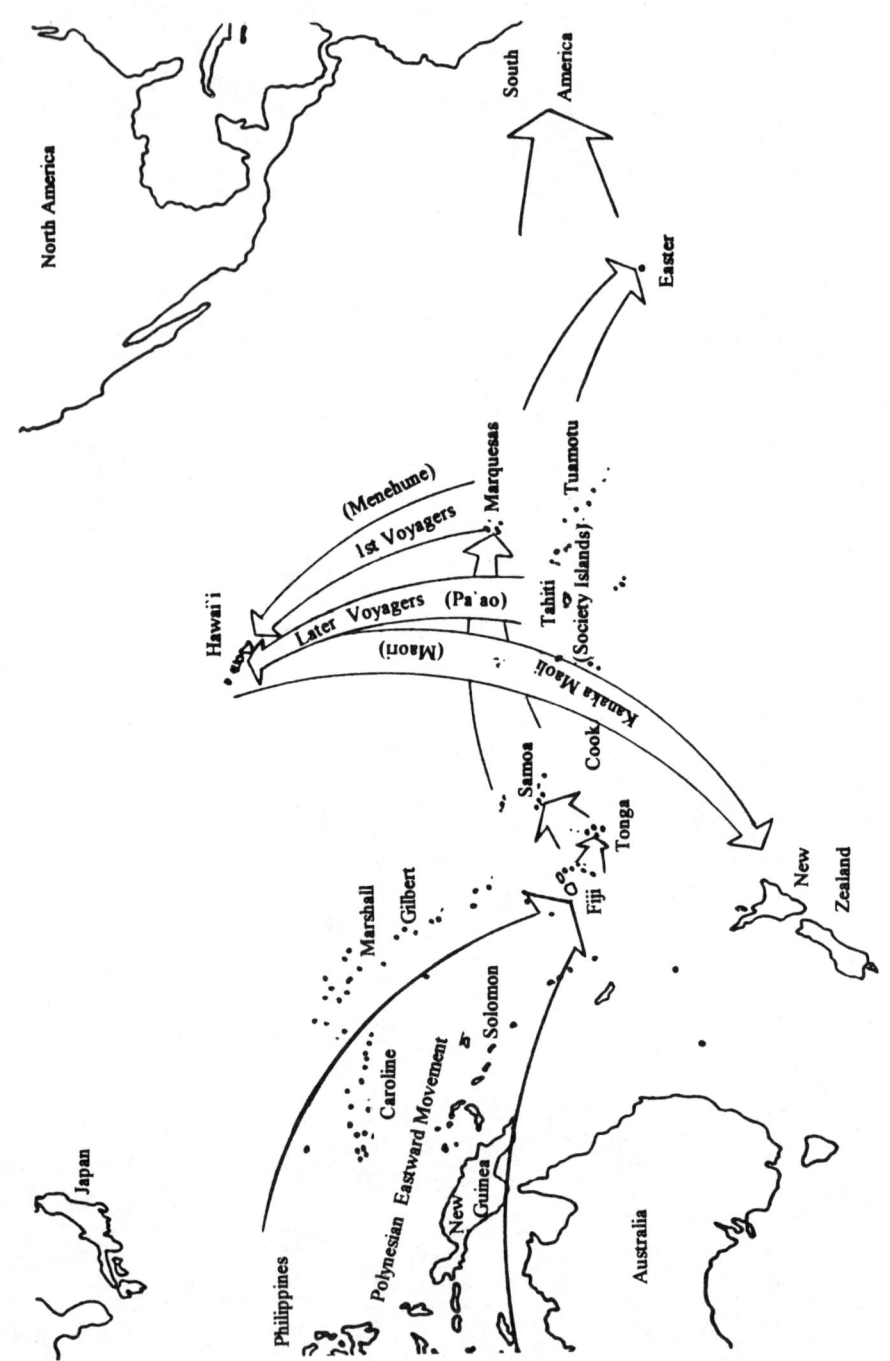

All dates are estimates from Biblical geneologies, legends and archeological evidence.

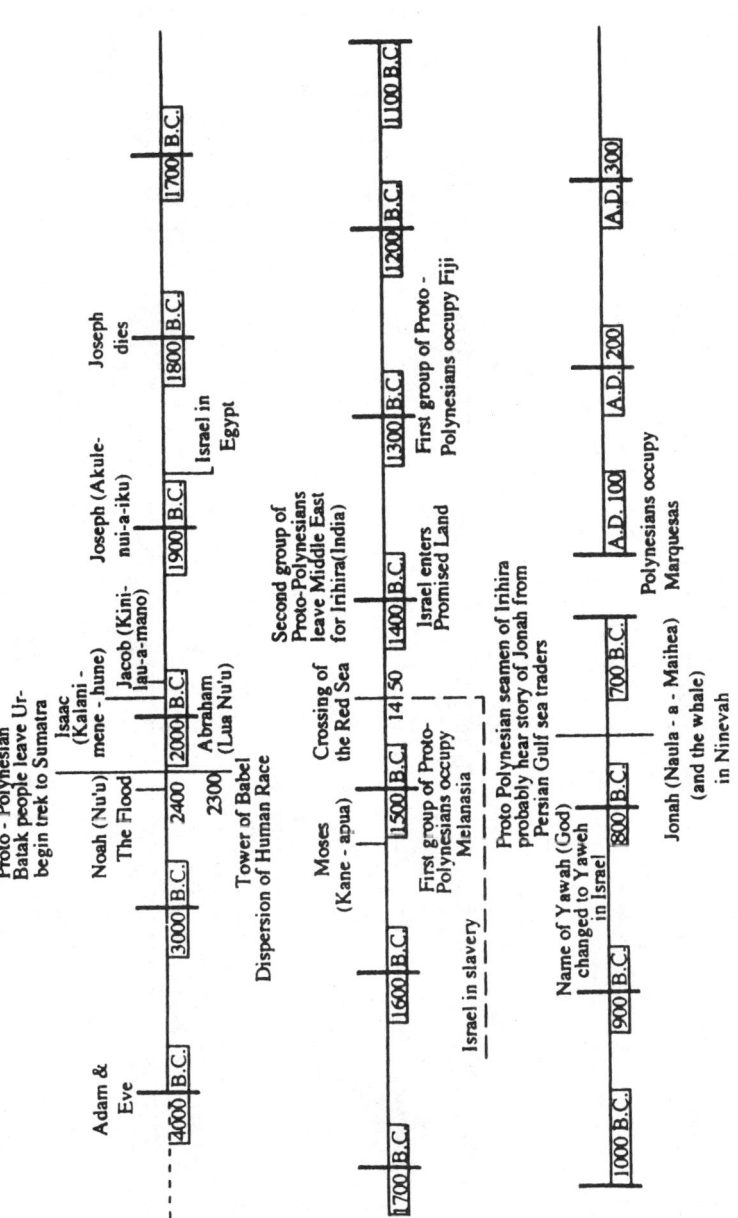

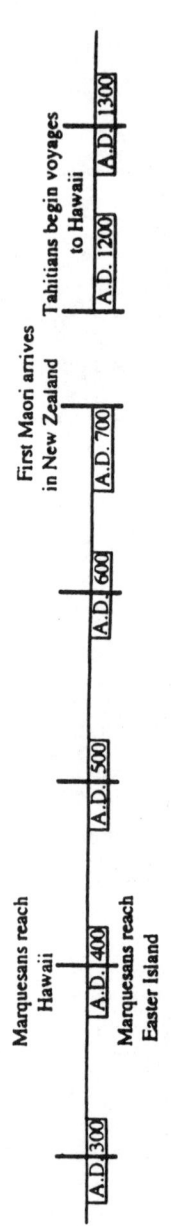

Marquesans reach
Hawaii

First Maori arrives
in New Zealand

Tahitians begin voyages
to Hawaii

| A.D. 300 | A.D. 400 | A.D. 500 | A.D. 600 | A.D. 700 | A.D. 1200 | A.D. 1300 |

Marquesans reach
Easter Island

| A.D. 1300 | A.D. 1400 | A.D. 1500 | A.D. 1600 | A.D. 1700 | A.D. 1800 |

Pa'ao arrives
in Hawaii

Maka'ainana (common people) suffer under Kapu system - - - - -

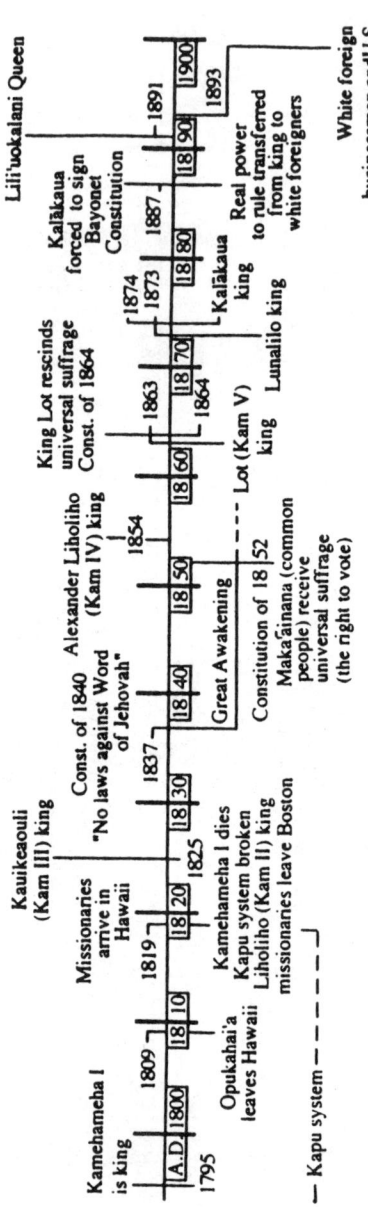

Li'luokalani Queen

Kalākaua
forced to sign
Bayonet
Constitution

Real power
to rule transferred
from king to
white foreigners

White foreign
businessmen and U.S.
Marines overthrow Queen

King Lot rescinds
universal suffrage
Const. of 1864

Kalākaua king

Lunalilo king

Alexander Liholiho
(Kam IV) king

Lot (Kam V)
king

Const. of 1840
"No laws against Word
of Jehovah"

Great Awakening

Constitution of 1852
Maka'ainana (common
people) receive
universal suffrage
(the right to vote)

Kauikeaouli
(Kam III) king

Missionaries
arrive in
Hawaii

Kamehameha I dies
Kapu system broken
Liholiho (Kam II) king
missionaries leave Boston

Kamehameha I is king

Opukahai'a
leaves Hawaii

| A.D. 1800 | 1810 | 1820 | 1830 | 1840 | 1850 | 1860 | 1870 | 1880 | 1890 | 1900 |

1795 1809 1819 1825 1837 1854 1863 1864 1873 1874 1887 1891 1893

— Kapu system - - - - -

Chapter 1

THE ONE TRUE GOD
OF POLYNESIA

". . . *the majority indeed, whose religion is truly monotheistic. These are the (Southern) Andamanese, probably the Kalinga Negritos, most of the Ituri pygmy groups, probably the Southwest Kivu Batwa, the Northeast Bushmen, part of the Northwest Bushmen, and especially the group we know most about, the Gabun pygmies. This means practically all of the African pygmies are monotheistic. . . . The ethnologically oldest groups, therefore, in the culture circle which embraces pygmy and pygmoid groups both are those which have preserved the purest and the strongest form of monotheism more perfectly and totally; . . . The pygmy and pygmoid groups both in Asia and in Africa, taken singly or together, originally possessed a thorough-going, clear and definite monotheism, . . .*"

Wilhelm Schmidt
Ernest Brandewie, translation

"There is no need to postulate any such relationship to explain the origins of the Viracocha cult. Behind the 'venerable Lord, the distant Lord, the most excellent Lord' we can distinguish a figure familiar to us in the mythology of every Indian tribe from Alaska to Tierra del Fuego. He is the 'Old Man of the Sky,' the 'Maker of Earth,' 'The Ancient One'; world creator and culture hero."

Alfred Metraux
History of the Incas

In the face of overwhelming evidence, many anthropologists now believe that primitive cultures began with a belief in <u>one supreme God</u>.[14] The Polynesian people have shown this to be true in their culture.

HOW THE POLYNESIAN ACCOUNTS WERE RECORDED

For a people with no written language, the Polynesian people have kept their legends and genealogies amazingly intact. In Hawai'i, most of the corruption seems to have occurred after the arrival of *Pa'ao* (an ancient Hawaiian priest) 700 - 900 years ago. Fortunately, in the late 1800's and early 1900's, several historians recorded what was left of the ancient oral histories of the Polynesian people. Although embellished and corrupted over time, many of the ancient accounts reflect the basic story that is found in Genesis 1-11.

A large volume of these accounts was preserved by a historian named *Abraham Fornander*. Martha Beckwith, one of the leading authorities on ancient Hawaiian history herself, says, "*As Malo is our most reliable native source for ancient practices, so Fornander is the leading foreign authority.*"[15] Fornander arrived in Hawai'i shortly after the missionaries and realized almost immediately that the missionaries were replacing the Hawaiian culture with their own. Through his wife, an *ali'i* (chieftess) of Moloka'i, he became appreciative of the beauty of this rapidly dying culture. *Kamehameha V* saw that Fornander loved the Hawaiian culture and that he had an extensive knowledge of the Hawaiian language. He, therefore, appointed him to "*find the old Hawai'i*" and record it before it was gone. Kamehameha also appointed the future king, *David Kalākaua*, and the future queen *Lili'uokalani*, his two best scholars, to assist him. Fornander was led by Kalākaua into the back country that was untouched by western culture. Accompanied by this high ali'i and with Kamehameha's edict, Fornander was allowed to hear sacred traditions of the deep past that were never recorded before.[16]

In the sections of the very ancient Hawaiian history, this author will frequently use the ancient accounts of the various other Polynesian peoples. Many of the very ancient accounts of Polynesian peoples were much alike. This indicates that they were common to the Polynesians before they separated and spread to their various islands. The Polynesian people — the Hawaiians, Tahitians, Samoans, Tongans, Marquesans, and Maori, to name the major people groups — are very close "cousins." In this section on the ancient Hawaiian legends, we will attempt to "*glean*," as Fornander put it, the "*Shreds of a purer cult . . . still preserved, soiled in appearance and obscured in sense by the contact, . . . yet standing on the traditional records as heirlooms of the past, as witnesses of a better creed.*"[17] In the sections of the ancient Hawaiian history, we will be using only the most accurate legends of the many similar legends available. The author would also like to make clear here that he has used the Bible as the measuring stick of accuracy (If the reader does not believe that the Bible is worthy of being the measuring stick of accuracy, the author would recommend reading, *Evidence That Demands A Verdict*, volumes 1 & 2 and *Scientific Creationism*). At times, we will also use parts of more corrupted versions that contain some important truth. Let's compare some of these accounts with the accounts given in Genesis 1-11.

'IO THE ONE TRUE GOD AND GENESIS I

Genesis 1:1 says, "*In the beginning God created the heaven and the earth.*" The Bible indicates that God is a Trinity of Father, Son, and Holy Spirit (Matthew 28:19, 2nd Corinthians 13:14). Genesis 1:26 says, "And God said, *Let us make man in our image, after our likeness . . .* " As God is three separate aspects working as one, so is man in three parts as one: body, soul and spirit. (1st Thessalonians 5:23) The Maori called the three parts of man, *tinana* (body), *mauri* (soul), and *wairua* (spirit).[18]

Fornander said, ". . . *I learn that the ancient Hawaiians at one time believed in and worshipped one god, comprising three beings, and respectively called Kāne, Kū and Lono, equal in nature, but distinct in attributes. . .*"

An ancient Marquesan chant says:

"O the princely son, first born of divine power!
O the Lord of everything, here, there, and always.
O the Lord of the heavens and the entire sky.
O the princely son, first born of the exalted power.
O the son, equal with the father and with Ono (the
spirit).
Dwelling in the same place.
Joined are they three in the same power.
The Father, Ono, and the Son."[19]

The Hawaiian word for eternity is *manawakolu*, meaning the *era of the three of divine power* (*mana* - divine power, *wa* - era and *kolu* - three).[20] The Hawaiian trinity was worshiped as one under many grand and mysterious names. As Wilhelm Schmidt describes, in many cases periphrases are substituted for the name of the Supreme Being. Some of these names in Hawai'i were *Hika-po-loa, Hika of the Long Night*; *Oi-e* signifying *Most Excellent Supreme; Ili-o-mea-lani* meaning *The Reflection of That Chiefly Someone*; *Kue-manu-ai-lehua*, literally *The Beak That Feeds on Lehuas* but meaning *The Power of Death*; *Uli* meaning *Eternity, Beyond Vision* and *Kū-kauhai*, meaning *The One Established.*[21]* These names were titles of the One True God, his true name being too sacred to mention; his name was *'Io.*

The author does not profess to be an expert in the Polynesian languages.
Therefore, in this book he simply relays the meanings of the words given
by the experts. Those people who heard the words, saw the facial
expressions and hand motions that accompanied them, heard their
intonation and received their meanings directly from the giver of the chant
or legend. He also does not include the Hawaiian markings, the "okina"
(glottal stop) or the "kahako" (macron) on any Hawaiian words on which
the emphasis is in doubt. A mark in the wrong place can change the
meaning of the word completely. The Hawaiian language has more words

with multiple meanings than almost any other language. Meanings of the words have also changed over time.[22] *Therefore, the author has deferred to the oldest, most direct and expert source wherever meanings of ancient words were concerned.*

The Maori legends say that 'Io dwelt in the uppermost of 12 heavens and was served by angelic beings who also acted as messengers.[23] Fornander said the Hawaiian legends relate that the triune God created three heavens, the earth to be their footstool (*he ke 'ehina honua-a-Kane*), and a host of angels or spirits (*i kini akua*) to minister to them.[24] Isaiah 66:1a says, "*Thus saith the Lord, the heaven is my throne, and the earth is my footstool . . .*" Unlike other Polynesian gods, no images were ever made of 'Io. This was similar to the Hebrew God, *Yahweh* of whom no image was made. Spirit beings entered the realm of 'Io through *Te Ara-tiatia*, meaning the way of steps. This entrance was also called *Te Toi-huarewa*, signifying a dangling or floating way or the idea of a suspended rope.[25] This is reminiscent of Jacob's ladder described in Genesis 28:12, "*And he dreamed, and behold a ladder set up on the earth, and the top of it reached to heaven: and behold the angels of God ascending and descending on it.*"

Abraham Fornander says that "*although grosser idolatry and cruel practices sprung from these beliefs in subsequent ages, these shreds of a purer cult were still preserved, heirlooms of the past that witnessed of a better creed.*" He also said that the chants to the triune Creator God were ". . . *specimens of the archaic simplicity of the language, hardly intelligible to the present Hawaiians.*"[26] *Mary Kawena Pukui*, one of the most respected scholars of ancient Hawaiian culture, says that *Pa'ao* (an ancient Hawaiian priest) introduced the warlike, vengeful aspects of the god Kū. She also says that, before Pa'ao's arrival, the gods were benign.[27] The Hawaiian historian, *Kepelino*, relates that Pa'ao instituted the severe religious observances which built up the power of the chiefs and priests. This occurred during the last period of migration to Hawai'i from the south. He also says that all of the old kahunas (priests) were put to death during this time.[28] Very little is known of this ancient triune God because most of the old priests were destroyed.

There is another reason little is known about 'Io; the name of this God of the Polynesians was too sacred to be mentioned openly. This was also true of the Israelites' God, Yahweh. This is why the Israelites also called their God by periphrases, like *Elohim* (God Almighty) or *Adonai* (Lord). This is not unusual. The ancient name of the One True God of *Aneityum* (New Hebrides), Nigeria, the *Yezidis* (Turkey), the Incas, the Navaho and other ancient cultures also were not openly mentioned.[29] The priests of Polynesia were under oath not to tell of the most sacred things, and the penalty for breaking this oath was death. The Polynesian authority, E. Handy, says that it is doubtful that the common folk were even allowed to know the true name of the Supreme Being.[30]

This was not an unusual situation. In ancient Babylon at one time, the priests were monotheistic and the people were polytheistic as it was in Polynesia.[31] This was also the situation with the ancient Chinese, Nigerians, Incas, and other peoples. It is easy then to understand why there is only a vague knowledge of the Supreme God in Hawaii. The priests of 'Io who would not be corrupted were either killed by the invader, Pa'ao, forced to worship in absolute secrecy or flee the islands. The commoners, on the other hand, didn't even know theSupreme God's name! Most of the Hawaiian researchers' materials that the author has read shows that the Hawaiians had no knowledge of 'Io. This is similar to the findings of the first Maori researchers, who said that the Maori only worshipped mountains, rocks and other natural things. The knowledge of 'Io had been hidden from them. A few Hawaiian Historians have revealed their knowledge of 'Io and a few trusted foreign Historians have been entrusted with this knowledge. The oral histories of a few acquaintances of the author confirm also, that a knowledge of 'Io was retained, albeit distorted by years of secrecy and veiled language. This knowledge of 'Io is vague and mysterious.

The most detailed knowledge of 'Io in Hawai'i was revealed by Emma Ahuena Taylor, a descendant of one of the priesthoods of 'Io, in 1931. She admitted however, that the knowledge of the families of the priesthood of 'Io who remained in Hawai'i was limited and only broken fragments remained.[32] She told of 'Io leaving Hawai'i with the chieftain *Hema* when he left for New Zealand.[33] Her ancestor, *Kahaku'i*, was the tutor of *Kamehameha the Great* when he was young. Kamehameha was the only one with the audacity to blaspheme the name of 'Io by mentioning it openly. He named his son *Liholiho 'Iolani*. The name 'Iolani was then given to Liholiho's grand nephew, Alexander Liholiho, who then named the royal palace 'Iolani. Ahuena attributes the extinction of the royal family and of the monarchy to this sacrilege by the royal family.[34]

Many of the chants to 'Io that remain are couched in double meanings. Most Hawaiian words had several layers of meanings ranging from the literal, "surface" meaning to the *kaona*, the deep, hidden or veiled meaning. On the surface, many chants to 'Io were outwardly about the owl and the hawk. The owl was symbolic of 'Io because he could see at night. The hawk was the highest flying and most powerful bird in the Hawaiian islands. These chants of the owl and the hawk are all that Hawaiian historians Malo, Mary Kawena Pukui, and a few others revealed. E.S.C. Handy, a well known researcher for the Bishop Museum, was shown chants to 'Io by another descendant of the priesthood of 'Io. This person regarded them too sacred to be published. The information that he collected and was allowed to publish are recorded in the Journal of the Polynesian Society.[35]

The author was privileged to have an interview with "Auntie" Malia Craver. Auntie Malia spoke Hawaiian as a first language and learned many things from her *kupuna* (elders). Her mentor was the most respected Hawaiian authority of modern times, Mary Kawena Pukui. Antie Malia told the author that although her kupuna worshipped the Supreme Being, 'Io, daily and taught her to do the same, they rarely mentioned their belief in 'Io to those outside of the *'ohana* (family). Until this day, Auntie Malia does not speak of 'Io unless asked specifically about him and only if she can see that the person will not belittle her God. She said that when Christianity came to Hawai'i, there was confusion in the 'ohana because they already had a Supreme Being. In an interview in the *'Iolani* Newspaper, Malia related that her ancestors said, "*Hele no kākou i ka pule a ho'olohe i ke kahuna pule i na he maika'i a pololei kona a'o ana e pili ana i ke Akua mana, o kēia ao nei mālama no kākou. I na oia e ho'opunipuni a ho'onui i kona Akua mamua o ko kākou he hewa no oia. He Akua 'ike a mana ko kākou lāhui Hawai'i mai kinohi a hiki i nēia lā.- Let us go to this church and listen to their minister. If it is good and they are right in their teaching about their powerful God of the universe, then we will keep that same God. The reason is that we have a God like theirs. If they are exaggerating that their God is better than our God, then they are wrong. We Hawaiians have had a powerful and all-knowing God from the beginning and until today.*"[36] Her kupuna accepted Jehovah but never told the missionaries about 'Io because they knew that their God would be ridiculed and called the devil by the missionaries. However, she would hear her Kupuna say while praying, "*Jehovah, you are 'Io.*"

The Navajo Indians also never mentioned their One True God to the "white man." Steve Watkins, a friend of Don Richardson (best selling author and linguist), grew up among the Navajo. He was well accepted by them and spoke their language, but he had never heard the Navajo mention the One Creator God. When queried about it by Don, Steve said he was positive that the Navajo never believed in One Creator God. However, urged by Don, he returned to the Four Corners Navajo Reservation to ask the medicine man about it. Steve asked the medicine man if the Navajo had One Creator God and was shocked when the medicine man said "yes!" Hurt, he asked the medicine man why he had never heard the name of this God mentioned even though he had grown up among them and was accepted by them. The medicine man replied that the Navajo elders had gathered together long ago and decided never to reveal the name of their God to the white man. He said that they had decided this because their God was so sacred and precious to them that they could not bear to have the white man belittle, laugh at, ridicule, or call their God the devil. After making him promise not to reveal the name of their precious God, Steve was told the name by the medicine man. True to his promise, Steve has never revealed the name, but the translation of that name is *The Glorious One Who Travels Alone*.

Kahu (Pastor) Ken Kekoa talked about 'Io on his television program. Several persons of Hawaiian ancestry called him afterwards. These people all had similar stories to tell. After hearing Ken speak of 'Io on the program, they went to their kupuna (elders) and asked them if this was true. These people all got similar answers. They were told, "*Shush! These things are not to be spoken about!*"

A friend of the author was told by her *kumu hula* (hula teacher), that 'Io was a god who was half bird and half man. He was even greater than the four major Hawaiian gods (Kāne, Kū, Lono and Kanaloa). This corruption of the knowledge of the One True God, after the extermination of the priestly guardians, is not unusual. It happened to the Incas who called the One True God, *Viracocha*. After the Spanish conquistadors obliterated the royal family and the upper class, Viracocha was corrupted into the sun god.[37]

The following are portions of a translated Maori sacred chant of creation compared to Genesis 1.

"*'Io dwelt within the breathing space of immensity. The universe was in darkness, with water everywhere. There was no glimmer of dawn, no clearness, no light. And he began by saying these words, that he might cease remaining inactive, 'Darkness, become a light-possessing darkness.' And at once light appeared.*"[38]

Genesis 1:2-3 says, "*And the earth was without form, and void; and darkness was upon the face of the deep. And the Spirit of God moved upon the face of the waters. And God said, Let there be light: and there was light.*"

"*. . . 'Io then looked to the waters which compassed him about and spake a fourth time, saying, 'Ye waters of Tai-kama, be ye separate. Heaven be formed.' Then the sky became suspended. 'Bring forth thou Tupu-horo-nuku.' And at once the moving earth lay stretched abroad.*"[39]

Genesis 1:6-9, *"And God said, Let there be a firmament in the midst of the waters, and let it divide the waters from the waters. And God made the firmament, and divided the waters which were under the firmament from the waters which were above the firmament: and it was so. And God called the firmament Heaven. And the evening and the morning were the second day. And God said, Let the waters under the heaven be gathered together unto one place, and let the dry land appear: and it was so."*

Recorded in the statutes of the Ming Dynasty are these words about the Chinese Creator, Shang Ti: *"Of old in the beginning, there was the great chaos, without form and dark. The five elements (planets) had not begun to revolve, nor the sun and moon to shine. You, O Spiritual sovereign first divided the grosser parts from the purer. You made heaven. You made earth. You made man. All things with their reproducing power got their being."*[40]

A Hindu, Brahminical account of creation recorded in the *"Analysis of the Code of Menu,"* published in the *"Asiatic Journal,"* Nov. 1827, says: *"The universe existed only in darkness, imperceptible, undefinable, as if wholly immersed in sleep. The self-existing power, himself undiscerned, with five elements and other principles, appeared in glory, dispelling the gloom. He, whom the mind alone can perceive, whose essence eludes the external organs, who has no visible parts, who exists from eternity, even he, the soul of all beings, whom no being can comprehend, shone forth in person.' Having willed to produce various beings from his own divine substance, first with a thought he created the waters; the*

waters are called nara, because they were the production of
Nara, or the spirit of God; and since they were his first
ayana, or place of motion, he thence is named Narayana, or
moving on the waters."[41]

THE NAMES OF 'IO

Sir Peter Buck says that the Maoris knowledge of 'Io
was held by an inner circle of priests who would not impart
this knowledge to the uninitiated. The knowledge of 'Io was
not known to the general public until the late 1850s when it
was revealed by the priest, *Te Matorohanga*. The knowledge
of 'Io as the Supreme Being and Creator was confined to the
highest order of priests who were called, *tohunga* (kahuna)
ahurewa.[42]

Buck counted 27 different names for 'Io.[43] A few of
these names and their meanings, listed below, are compared
with Biblical descriptions of God.

'Io-matua: he is the parent of all things, natural phenomena,
plants, animals, man, and gods.
Colossians 1:16 - "For by him were all things created, that
are in heaven, and that are in earth, visible and
invisible"

'Io-matua-kore: He had no parents, "he was nothing
but himself."
(Hebrew) Yahweh: meaning. The Self- existent One.
Exodus 3:14, "I AM THAT I AM."

'Io-te-wananga: He is the source of all knowledge.
>   Colossians 2:3 - "In whom are hid all the treasures
>   of wisdom and knowledge."

'Io-mata-ngaro: His face is hidden and unseen.
>   Exodus 33:20, "And he said, Thou canst not see my
>   face: for there shall no man see me, and live."

'Io-te-waiora: He is the source and giver of life.
>   Psalm 36:9, "For with thee is the fountain of life:"

'Io-mata-wai: 'Io, the God of love.
>   John 3:16, "For God so loved the world, that he
>   gave his only begotten Son, that whosoever
>   believeth in him should not perish, but have
>   everlasting life."

Because 'Io was so uncannily like the Hebrew God
Yahweh, some researchers thought that 'Io had evolved after
contact with Christian teaching. However, there are references
to 'Io in the literature of different Maori tribes well before the
Old Testament was introduced to New Zealand.[44] The
knowledge of 'Io has been uncovered in at least seven
different Maori tribes. This is a considerable amount when one
realizes that most priests of 'Io believed revealing this
knowledge meant death![45] The Maori authority, Best, says, "
. . . *a considerable amount of the ritual pertaining to this cult
has been preserved . . . much more than appears in vol. 3 of
the Memoirs of the Polynesian Society. Some of these have
been obtained by the writer, while others are preserved in
manuscript books in the possession of natives, which will
probably never be permanently recorded. All this matter is
couched in exceedingly archaic language, and it is impossible*

to believe that it has all been composed during late years."[46]

Davis, in the *Life and Times of Patuone*, published in 1876, writes, *"I have been informed by natives well acquainted with the ancient mode of worship among their people that the oldest Maori prayers were those addressed to the sacred 'Io."*[47] Best also records that ancient prayers to 'Io were also made by the Tahitians and Rarotongans " . . . *which disposes of the idea of a modern local invention. Collusion is out of the question.*"[48] The *Tuamotuans* (The *Tuamotus* are an island chain east of Tahiti.) also had a hidden high God called *Kiho.* The creation chants of *Kiho* are almost a duplicate of the Maori creation chants of 'Io. Stimson writes, *"These chants of Fariua's (Kiho chants) have been shown to leading sages from many sections of the Tuamotus, and all have expressed the unqualified opinion that they are genuine archaic compositions impossible of imitation in these days when the ancient modes of expression and even the meanings of the words themselves have become widely forgotten and often corrupted by the invading and now nearly universal Tahitian language. It is unlikely that there is a Tuomotuan native alive today capable of composing these, or similar, cosmogonic chants.*"[49] Many ancient peoples had creation accounts that paralleled the Genesis 1 account.

In the book, *History of the People of Israel, Vol. 1,* Ernest Renan states in the chapter *The Name of Iahveh* (Yahweh, Jehovah), that this holy name became contracted into *Iahou* or *Io!*[50] Renan was not a Christian nor did he have any knowledge of Polynesian Religion. The *Theological Wordbook of the Old Testament* confirm Renan, saying that the name of Yahweh was shortened to *yho* and *yo* when used in names.[51] This shortened name for the One True God is used in names like: *Joel (Ioel)* - 'Io (Yahweh) is God, *Jonathan*

(Ionathan) - 'Io (Yahweh) has given and *Joshua (Y'shua, Ioshua, Jesus* - Greek) - 'Io (Yahweh) saved. The *Yo* or *Jo* sound can only be pronounced in Hawaiian as *"Io."* The Hawaiian Bible, *Ka Baibala Hemolele*, translates these names as *'Ioela* (Joel), *'Ionakana* (Jonathan), *'Iosua* (Joshua). This is very similar to the Greek translation of these Hebrew names, *Ioel* (Joel) and *Ioannes* (John). The Greek for Joshua, Jesus, is taken from the unabbreviated form of this name, *Jehoshua* (Yehoshuwa) and is translated in the Greek as *Iesous*.

KĀNE

Kāne (*Tāne* in most of Polynesia, *Atea* in the Marquesas) was the aspect of the supreme being who was, in a sense, representative of the supreme being. He was the creator of all living things. Kāne was the heavenly father of all men and the creator of men. In this sense, the *Kāne* aspect of the triune God of Polynesia, corresponds to the *Son* aspect of God in the Bible. Many primitive Supreme Gods also relegated the task of creation to a subordinate being who was usually called the *First Father* or *Creator*.[52]

John 1:1-4 says of Jesus, *"In the beginning was the Word, and the Word was with God, and the Word was God. The same was in the beginning with God. All things were made by him, and without him was not any thing made that was made. In him was life; and the life was the light of men."*

An old Hawaiian prayer to Kāne says in part, *" . . . Life to the land! Life from Kāne, Kāne the god of life." "Life to the people! Hail Kāne of the water of life! Hail!"* The phrase, "*Kāne, the water of life,*" is often found in prayers to Kāne. A part of a long mele about the water of life published in Emerson's study of the Hula says, *"Where is the water of Kāne? At the Eastern Gate, where the sun comes in at Haehae; there is the water of Kāne." "...A water of magic power - the water of life! Life! O give us this life!"*[53]

It may be interesting to note that Ezekiel 43:1-2 says, *"Afterward he brought me to the gate, even the gate that looketh toward the east: And, behold, the glory of the God of Israel came from the way of the east: and his voice was like a noise of many waters: and the earth shined with his glory."* Revelations 22:1 also says, *"And he shewed me a pure river of water of life, clear as crystal, proceeding out of the throne of God and of the Lamb."* Other primitive religions also mentioned the"water of life."[54]

As time passed and corruption of the ancient accounts occurred, Kāne became known as the God of light and fresh water which are necessary for life.

LONO AND KŪ

There is very little left of the ancient traditions of *Kū* (or *Tū*) and *Lono* (*Ono, Rongo*). Perhaps *Kū* originally represented the *Father* aspect of God. Fornander says that he represented stability.[55] The aspect of the Father that metes out judgement may have later caused the god Kū to be corrupted into the god of war and judgement, calling for the death of those who broke the "law" (kapus).

Lono may have represented the Holy Spirit. A prayer offered to Lono during the *Makahiki* (the Hawaiian new year rites) says in part, *"Send gracious showers of rain, oh Lono, Life-giving rain, a grateful gift,"*[56] Lono's surname was *Noho i ka Wai* (dwelling on the water). Genesis 1:2b says, *"And the Spirit of God moved upon the face of the waters."* The Hindu Code of Menu quoted previously said, *". . . the waters are called nara, because they were the production of Nara, or the spirit of God; and since they were his first ayana, or place of motion, he thence is named Narayana, or moving on the waters."* An ancient Tahitian tradition says that, *"In the beginning there was nothing but the god Ihoiho; afterwards there was an expanse of waters which covered the abyss, and the god Tino Taata floated on the surface."*[57] An ancient Marquesan chant says, *"Ono, the Spirit."*[58]

Lono, more importantly, was the God of Peace. Indeed the Maori word for a peace treaty is *Rongo* (Lono).[59]

The god *Kanaloa* was never a part of the triune God. This god was added to the major gods of Hawai'i after the coming of Pa'ao. Kanaloa will be discussed in the following chapter.

THE PULO'ULO'U

The Hawaiian people also had the remnants of their worship of the One True God in the *Pulo'ulo'u*. The Pulo'ulo'u was a simple stick with a white tapa cloth ball at the end of it. Oral tradition collected by Calvin Kawailani Eaton relates that the round white ball represented the one supreme God. The white represented white light. The Pulo'ulo'u was later corrupted into the *Kapu Stick*, which separated the ali'i and the commoners.

CHAPTER 2

THE CREATION OF MAN

"In the great majority of peoples belonging to the primitive cultures, the typical figure which we find is that of the Supreme Being, who has neither wife nor family. Under him and created by him are the primal pair from whom the tribe is descended. We find this form among the Pygmies of Central Africa, the South-East Australians, the inhabitants of North Central California, the primitive Algonkins, and, to a certain extent, the Koryaks and the Ainu."

Wilhelm Schmidt
The Origin and Growth of Religion

THE FIRST MAN

There are many accounts in Polynesia of the creation of man. Some of them state that the supreme triune God made the heavens and the earth in six days and rested on the seventh day. This is exactly as stated in the book of Genesis. The legends also say that, last of all on the sixth day, the triune God created man in the likeness of Kāne. Hence, man is also called Kāne. (In the Marquesas, the first man is called *Atea* after the creator of men, Atea) The body of the man was made of red earth and his head of whitish clay mixed with the spittle of the gods. When the clay image of Kāne was ready, the three gods breathed into its nose and it became a living being.[60] Genesis 2:7 says, "*And the Lord God formed man of the dust of the ground, and breathed into his nostrils and man became a living soul.*" It is interesting that the word Adam in Hebrew (Aloros in Chaldean[61] and Adam in Phoenician[62]) means, "taken out of the red earth."[63] Many other legends of the creation of the first man (also called *Tiki* or *Ti'i*) and woman throughout Polynesia speak of them being created out of red clay by Tane (Kāne).

In many primitive religions the primal pair were made of clay. Among the *Kulin* of South-East Australia, the Supreme Being breathes life into the body made of clay through its nose, mouth and navel. *Gabon* Pygmy tradition states that the Supreme Being made the body of the first man of wet clay and gave it life by his almighty word.[64]

THE FIRST WOMAN

These legends also tell of the creation of the first woman. This woman was created from one of the ribs — *lalo puhaka* — of the man while he was asleep. These two were the progenitors of all mankind.[65] Genesis 2:21-22 says, "*And the Lord God caused a deep sleep to fall upon Adam, and he slept: and He took one of his ribs, and closed up the flesh instead thereof; And the rib, which the Lord God had taken from man, made He a woman, and brought her unto the man."*

Inscribed on an ancient Sumerian cylinder is the story of the first couple, *Enki* and *Ninhursag*, who were occupants of an earthly paradise. In this inscription, the first woman was also created from the rib of the man.[66]

The first man was called by many names in the various Hawaiian chants and legends. The most common name for the man was *Kumu-honua*, and the woman, *Ke ola kū honua*. All of the many names of the first man speak of the origin, happiness, greatness and power of this *ali'i* (chief). In the legend of *Wela-ahi-lani*, the man is called Wela-ahi-lani and the woman, *Owe*. The progenitors of the Marquesans are called *Atea* and *Owa*. In Tahitian the first female is *Iwi* who is taken from one of the bones of Ti'i, the first man. The word *iwi* in Tahiti and *ivi* in Samoa came to mean bone.[67] In Rotuma, she is known as *Iva*.[68] These names are amazingly close to the name given the woman in Genesis, *Eve*.

In his *Traditions of Hawai'i*, Kepelino translates three names of the man and woman.

The man:
1. Kumu Honua, meaning muddy soil;
2. Honua'ula, meaning red soil;
3. Kalepoahulu, meaning the first man of the soil;

The woman:
1. Lalohonua, meaning a side of Kumu Honua
2. Koloikeae, meaning propagation of life;

3.Laloheleae, meaning to reproduce[69]

A Tongan legend of the first man and woman says that they were still innocent and went about naked, for they were not ashamed.[70] Genesis 2:25 says, "*And they were both naked, the man and his wife, and were not ashamed.*"

Certain researchers of Hawaiian history over the years have doubted the authenticy of the Hawaiian creation accounts because of their striking similarity to the Biblical Genesis. However, these similarities are not unusual. Epics of Creation, found on tablets in the ruins of Babylon, Nineveh, Nippur and Ashur, also include all the main parts of the Genesis creation, as follows:

1. "in the beginning" a "primeval abyss," a"chaos of waters" called "the deep," the gods "formed all things"

2. The gods made "upper and lower firmaments"- "established the heavens and the earth"

3. "ordained the stars" on the fourth day

4. "made the grass and green herbs to grow"

5. made "the beasts of the field and the cattle and all living things"

6. on the 6th day, "formed man out of the dust of the ground," "they became living creatures" "man with wife they dwelt," "companions they were," "in a garden was their dwelling," "clothing they knew not"

7. The "7th" day was appointed a "holy day," "to cease from all business commanded"[71]

THE POLYNESIAN EDEN

The first man and woman dwelt in a place of great beauty also called by many names. One was, *Kalana i Hauola*, meaning *Kalana with the living* or *life-giving dew.*[72] A Maori legend says that at the time of the first man, there was no water.[73] It is interesting that Genesis 5-6 says ". . . *for the Lord God had not caused it to rain upon the earth, and there was not a man to till the ground. But there went up a mist from the earth, and watered the whole face of the ground."*

Other names for this place were, *Pali-uli, The Blue Mountain,"* '*Āina i ka Kaupo o Kāne*, the *Land in* or *of the Heart of Kāne*, '*Āina wai Akua a Kāne*, the *Land of the Divine Water of Kāne."* This place was situated on a continent also called by various names.[74]

"*He* (the Supreme Being) *also furthers the moral education of men inasmuch as He punishes the wrongs which He knows have occurred. In the present life He does this by sending sickness and death. On the other hand, He rewards people who observe His law with health and long life. . . This set of beliefs goes back to the very earliest common religion and is not, therefore, merely a regional variation. The first sin of man in "paradise" was punished, as far as the North Central Californians and the oldest Algonkians were concerned, with the entry of death and physical evil in the world."*

Wilhelm Schmidt
Ernest Brandewie, translation

THE FALL OF THE FIRST MAN AND WOMAN

The oral tradition of the *Proto-Polynesian* Karen people of Burma describe best how this fall occurred and how worshiping other gods began:

Tha-nai and *Ee-u* worshiped their creator in a beautiful garden. Their creator's name was *Y'wa*. They fell into sin when *Mu-kaw-lee* fooled the woman into eating of the forbidden fruit. Y'wa said to them, *"Why have you eaten the fruit of the tree that I commanded you not to eat? . . . therefore you shall grow old, and you shall become sick, and you shall die."* Mu-kaw-lee instructed them in the offerings he wanted for the different kinds of sickness to be healed. These offerings were to be made to his servants who were the lords over certain diseases, as well as accidents.[75]

In many primitive religions, the Supreme Being is opposed by another being who is the representation of evil. This being meets all the endeavors of the Supreme Being for good with protests and hindrances.[76]

In the Hawaiian paradise called Kalana i Hau-ola, there grew the *Ulu kapu a Kāne*, the forbidden bread-fruit tree, and the *'Ōhi'a Hemolele*, the sacred apple-tree. The ancient priests believed that the trouble and death of the first man and woman were connected to these trees. This was apparently corrupted over time by the Marquesans to necessitate human sacrifice. A Marquesan sacrificial chant frequently alludes to the *"red apples eaten in Naoau,"* and to the *"tabooed apples of Atea,"* as the cause of death, wars, pestilence, famine, and other calamities. The chant also says that *"these can only be atoned for by human sacrifice."*[77]

Also connected to this fall of the first man and woman was an animal called the *Mo'opeloa*. Mo'opeloa means *The Serpent of Lies* or *Flattery* (*Mo'o* - serpent, lizard or reptile and *pelo* - to flatter, tell tall tales or lie). *Mo'o* not only means *lizard* in Samoan but can mean *envy*.[78] This crafty and lying reptile was also known as *Ilioha*. A part of this chant says, "*The Ilioha, mischief-maker, stands on the land; He has caught the chief Kū-Honua, and Polo-Haina, the woman, the tabu chiefs of Kāne . . .* " Another part of this ancient chant reads:

> "*O Kāne-La'a-'uli, uli, uli,*
> *dead by the feast, feast, feast,*
> *dead by the oath, by the law, law, law,*
> *truly, thus indeed, dead, dead, dead.*
>
> *...And cursed be my hand,*
> *cut off be my course!*
> *E Kāne-La'a-'uli, uli, uli,*
> *E Kāne-La'a-huli, huli, huli,*
> *E Kāne-La'a-make, make, make,*
> *dead are you, you, you,*
> *by Kāne thy god, god, god,*
> *dead by the law, law, law,*
> *truly thus indeed, dead, dead, dead,*
> *O Kāne-La'a-'uli, uli, uli,*
> *O Kāne disobeying the gods, gods, gods,*
> *O Kāne (returned) to dust, dust, dust.*"[79]

"Genesis 3:17 & 19 says, "*And unto Adam he (God) said, Because thou hast hearkened unto the voice of thy wife, and hast eaten of the tree, of which I commanded thee, saying, Thou shalt not eat of it: cursed is the ground for thy sake; in sorrow shalt thou eat of it all the days of thy life; ...In the sweat of thy face shalt thou eat bread, till thou return unto the ground; for out of it wast thou taken: for dust thou art, and unto dust shalt thou return."*

KANALOA

Another account of this event says that *Kanaloa* was the leader of the first company of spirits made after the earth was separated from heaven. These spirits were not made like man but were the servants or messengers of the gods. These spirits, according to the Hawaiiana authority M. Beckwith, were "*spit out by the gods.*"

The anthropologist G. Smith recorded a Chaldean account which said that seven spirits rebelled against *Anu* (one of the three creation gods of the Chaldeans). They spread consternation in heaven and destruction on earth but were finally conquered by *El* (*El* is also the creation God of the Canaanites) the son of *Ea* (the third god of their creation trinity).[80]

The Hawaiian account says that these messengers of the gods rebelled, led by Kanaloa, because they were not allowed to drink *'awa* ('awa implies worship). They were defeated by Kāne and cast down to the underworld where Kanaloa, also known as *Milu*, became the ruler of the dead. Milu appears as *Miru* in central Polynesia and Southern New Zealand and also as *Whiro* whose manifestation was a lizard (*mo'o*).[81]

This legend speaks of Kāne desiring good for man and Kanaloa, evil. When Kāne drew the figure of a man in the earth, Kanaloa made one also. Kāne's man lived but Kanaloa's did not. Kanaloa was angry, cursed man to die and made all kinds of poisonous things. In New Zealand, Tangaroa is not only the god of the ocean but of reptiles. (Tangaroa may have become the god of the ocean because he was the god of the "deep") The Maoris represent death as a lizard and believe a person becomes ill because someone has dispatched a *ngarara* (reptile, monster, lizard) against them. A Tainui Maori chant says in part, "*Crush in the head of the demon, Death! The Dragon that consumes all mankind!*"[82] Like Satan in the Biblical account, Kanaloa seduces the wife of the first man in the form of a serpent.[83]

In the very ancient accounts, Kanaloa was never mentioned in conjunction with the trinity of major gods. His inclusion as one of the great gods of Hawai'i can only be traced to the last waves of Polynesian voyagers from Tahiti.

Kanaloa was called, in the Kumulipo, the evil smelling squid, *Ka-he'e-hauna-wela*. According to the Hawaiian historian, Kepelino, Kanaloa was the personified spirit of evil, the originator of death, and the prince of *Po* (Darkness or the Void). The Hawaiian legends spoke of three Pos. The Po of Milu (Kanaloa), was a place of "*unending fire and of strange impenetrable darkness*". It was a place where the spirits of the people who fall there were "*lost and they became hideous.*" It was "*death without measure, night without measure, weeping without measure, and the dwelling place without end.*"[84] In the Tuamotus, ancient traditions relate the earth is composed of three separate strata. the uppermost stratum was destined for fortunate souls or spirits; the middle was for the living, and the lowest was a place where spirits wandered in pain.[85]

The Rig Veda says, "*Heaven is a place where light is perpetual. It is a beautiful place where there is happiness, pleasures, joy and enlightenment.*" It also says that hell is the place of eternal death and eternal punishment. It is a deep pit and a place of darkness where the wicked fall down headlong.[86]

Schmidt writes *"All primitive peoples without exception believe in another life."* The good go to a paradise or heaven while *"The lot of the wicked is often described expressly as one of painful punishment, by fire and heat, as among the Ajongo Negrillos and the Souther Wiradyuri; but it may also be by cold, or by wanderings without rest."*[87]

Schmidt also writes that, *"This belief in endless reward or punishment due the soul because of the way the individual conducted himself morally in this life is so widespread and characteristic in all of the ancient cultures, that it must have been a fundamental part of the oldest common religion and part of a moral code common to all."*

Kanaloa (Hawai'i), Tangaloa (Tonga and Samoa) or Ta'aroa (Tahiti), was the supreme being and creator in Tonga, Samoa and Tahiti. Handy believes that this Kanaloa cult was introduced to these islands by a later migration of people. He says:

> *"The hypothesis that Tangaloa was introduced later than Tu, Tane, and Rongo is alone capable of explaining his position in different sections of Polynesia. In the three main groups of islands on the outer margin of this area (Hawai'i, the Marquesas, New Zealand) he appears in the genealogies as a descendant from the marriage of Heaven and Earth. He was also a deity of prime importance in both mythology and worship, <u>but was never elevated to the position of creator.</u> On the other hand, in the three main groups in the central and western region of*

Polynesia (Samoa, Tonga, and the Society Islands) he was regarded as the preexistent Supreme Being who originated all things."[88](author's emphasis)

This hypothesis is supported by the fact that the Tahitians did know of 'Io. 'Io's full name being, *'Io-i-te Vahinaro*, meaning, *'Io at the Hidden Place.*[89] They also had a tradition that "*In the beginning there was nothing but the God Ihoiho; afterwards there was an expanse of waters which covered the abyss, and the god Tino Taata floated on the surface.*"[90] This again closely parallels Genesis 1:1-2.

As mentioned earlier, the Tangaloa cult almost totally supplanted the former religion in Central and Western Polynesia. When it was later brought by the Tahitians to Hawai'i, however, it mixed with the Hawaiian legends. This is why legends of creation in Hawai'i relate totally different accounts of the beginning of the world and mankind. This also explains why some legends portray Kanaloa as the personification of evil and some do not.

Fornander said, "*That the Marquesan Tanaoa and the Hawaiian Kanaloa embody the same original conception of evil, I consider pretty evident.*"[91] (Kanaloa is also a Polynesian family name and an actual person in the genealogies of many Polynesians. These are not to be confused with the god Kanaloa).

An ancient Marquesan chant says "*Sprang up wars, fierce and long. Atea* (One name of the Marquesan creation God and the name of the first man created in his image. Atea also meant light.) *and Tanaoa* (darkness), *great wrath and contention . . . Tanaoa confined, . . . O thrones whereon to seat the Lord of love* (Atea); *The great Lord Atea established in love . . . Atea gave nothing back to Tanaoa, Who thus was chased to distant regions, Where the light of day was not known; . . . O dark Tanaoa engulfed in the long nights.*"[92]

Kanaloa poses as the supreme being and creator in Central and Western Polynesia. However, he shows his true colors, as the evil serpent who is constantly trying to control man and deceive him into worshiping him, in this official chant for the casting off of a "god" (demon) of Kanaloa. Kanaloa is spoken of as *Ta'aroa* in this Tahitian chant.

> *"There is a casting off, I am casting thee off. Do not come in to possess me again; let me not be a seat for thee again! Let me not know thee again; do thou not know me again. Go and seek some other medium for thyself in another home. Let it not be me, not at all! I am wearied of thee-I am terrified with thee! I am expelling thee. Go ever to the Vai-tu-po (River-in-darkness), into the presence of Ta'aroa, thy father, Ta'aroa, the father of all gods. Return not again to me. Behold the family, they are stricken with sickness; thou art taking them, thou art a terrible man-devouring god.*"[93]

How different this is from the Supreme Beings Atea, Lord of Love and 'Io-mata-wai, the God of Love!

THE EFFECTS OF THE FALL

After this fall, the names of this first man and woman were changed from expressions of happiness, joy and power to names denoting misfortune, remorse and grief. The new names of the couple had meanings like *Fallen, Tree-eater, Tree-upset, Mourner* and *Lamentation*. After the fall, the name of the woman preceded the name of the man in this chant. Hawaiian tradition says that this pair was driven out of paradise by *Ka-ʻaʻaia-nūkea-nui a Kāne*, the large white bird of Kāne. This may represent the angel mentioned in Genesis 1.[94]

CHAPTER 3

THE GREAT FLOOD

"Among the traditions preserved from remote ages by the human race, there are perhaps none more important to the ethnologist than those which relate, in every great district of the world, and with so much unity combined with so much variety, the occurrence of a great Deluge in long past time."[95]

Edward Tylor
Researches Into the Early History of Mankind and the Development of Civilization

Many peoples have accounts of the great flood, among these are the Babylonians, Sumerians, Assyrian, Persians, Egyptians, Greeks, Hindus, Chinese, Druids, Mexicans, Peruvians, American Indians, Australians, Greenlanders, Fijians and Polynesians.[96] Although many accounts of this ancient event have been distorted, they still point toward a common beginning.

BETWEEN THE FALL AND THE FLOOD

In Polynesian history, as in the histories of the Chaldees and Hebrews, there is little mention of the events between the fall of the first man and the time of the great flood. It may be interesting to note however, that the Polynesian legends account for three sons of the first man. Of these, the second son was murdered by the first. This is the same as the Biblical account where Cain kills Abel (Genesis 4).

As in the Biblical and other ancient accounts, the length of years that a man lived was also enormous. Kumuhonua was said to have lived to see his children's children increase and fill the earth. His days, however, were filled with grief and sorrow because he had not kept the law commanded him by Kāne. The Polynesian accounts also speak of the translation of worthy individuals (those who lived pious lives) to heaven. There are two in Polynesian accounts and one, Enoch, in the Hebrew.[97]

THE POLYNESIAN NOAH

The next in-depth historical account, in both the Hebrew and Polynesian traditions, is the story of the Great Flood. The hero of the Great Flood in Polynesia was called *Nuʻu* and his wife, *Lili-Noe*. The name, Nuʻu, is very similar to the Hebrew and Arabic names for this man, *Nuh* or Noah. Kumuhonua is said to have lived almost to the time of Nuʻu.

One Maori flood legend says that at the time of the flood, men had become very numerous on the earth. There were many great tribes, evil prevailed everywhere, the tribes quarreled and wars were frequent, the worship of Tāne (Kāne) was neglected and his doctrines openly denied.[98] It is also said in Hawaiian tradition, that the time of Nuʻu was a time of wickedness. The One True God was jealous because the people turned to evil doings, so he punished all men by the flood.[99]

The Polynesian legends speak of Nuʻu building a large vessel with a house on top of it or of Kāne giving Nuʻu the vessel, called in some Hawaiian chants, *"Canoe Like a Chief's House"* or *"Great Canoe of Kāne."* The Polynesian legends shed light on a dispute among Biblical scholars. Some believe that the dimensions of the Ark given in Genesis 6:14-16 are the actual dimensions of the boat. Others believe that these were the dimensions given for the living space inside of the Ark. The Polynesian legends describing a large vessel with a house on top of it seems to validate the second viewpoint.

In Genesis 7:4, Noah was given seven days notice by God of the coming flood. Nuʻu was also given seven days notice by his God. According to the Marquesan chant *Te-Tai-Toko*, which seems to be the least corrupted of the various flood legends, this house had stories and chambers with openings for light. Genesis 6:16 says *"A window shalt thou make to the ark . . . with lower, second, and third stories shalt thou make it."* It was also stored with provisions for the preservation of various animals. The animals were fastened with ropes, tied up in couples, and marched into the vessel. The people saved in this vessel were Nuʻu, his three sons, and their wives. This makes a total of eight people saved, the same as mentioned in the Bible.[100]

In the *Epic of Gilgamesh, Utnapishtim,* the Babylonian Noah says, *"All I had of silver I loaded, all I had of gold I loaded, all I had of the seed of all living creatures*

I loaded; I made all my kin and family go into the boat. The animals of the fields, the beasts of the field, the children of all the craftsmen I drove aboard." XI, 80-86.

   Utnapishtim said after the rain had stopped, *"The storm was over and the rain of destruction had ceased. I looked forth. I called aloud over the waters . . . The sunlight suffused my countenance. I was dazzled and sank down weeping, and the tears streamed over my face. Everywhere I looked I saw water!"*[101]

   Kepelino translated a prayer called the *Prayer of the Pleasure-Lover*. This prayer was made by a brother-in-law of Nu'u who was a wicked man. At the time when Nu'u and his family entered the *Canoe Like a Chief's House* and closed the door, this brother-in-law was indulging himself with pleasures. The water came from above and the ocean also came up. The land was covered and the people were in distress. Then this wicked brother-in-law ran and tried to enter the great canoe. He called to those inside but was not heard. He then besought Lono in the name of his sister. When this tactic did not work, he began to spew curses. He called upon Lono to destroy the whole earth. He prayed that Lalo-Honua (the first woman), called *Kahuli* in the chant, and Kumu-Honua (the first man), called *Lepo-Ahulu* in the chant, might live again. He wanted Kumu-Honua to see with his own eyes the terrible trouble he had caused and to die again with them in this punishment brought about by his disobedience.[102]

   After the flood, as dry land started to appear, Nu'u sent out a bird of dark color (a raven in the Biblical account). Next Nu'u sent out another bird (a dove in the Biblical account) which returned with branches it had gathered. As with Noah in the Bible, Nu'u offered a sacrifice to his God when he landed. Nu'u saw the moon and thinking that it was

Kāne, worshiped it. Kāne then descended on a rainbow and
reproved Nuʻu for his mistake. Nuʻu then asks for forgiveness
and Kāne forgives him, leaving the rainbow as a token of his
forgiveness.[103] Pei Te Hurinui said in the Tainui Maori, House
of Sacred Learning, it was taught that "*Kahukura Uenuku was
set up as a symbol to man of the godhood of ʻIo. ʻIo was so
intensely sacred in himself that even the utterance of his
name was avoided on all ordinary occasions. This is the
reason why it was laid down that only to his symbol, Uenuku
(the rainbow) were the common people to sing their sacred
chants. It was the prerogative of the altar priests to recite the
sacred chants to ʻIo.*"[104] In some accounts, Nuʻu landed in an
expansive country called *Kahiki-honua-kele* and dwelt
there.[105]

Nuʻu and his wife also had different names:

Nuʻu
   1. *Nuʻu,* meaning a new ancestor;

   2. *Nuʻu Pule,* meaning praying Nuʻu;
   3. *Nuʻu Kahuna,* meaning Nuʻu the priest
      or sacrificing Nuʻu;
   4. *Nuʻu o Kāne,* meaning Nuʻu close to God.

Nuʻu's wife
   1. *Nuʻumea,* meaning the female Nuʻu
      who propagates;
   2. *Nuʻumealani,* meaning the female Nuʻu who
      prays
   3. *Luanuʻu,* meaning the female Nuʻu of the
      new generation that dies;

4. *Lilinoe*, meaning the end of punishment and
the cessation of anger.[106]

In the Maori, Nu'u is called *Nuku*. The word Nuku has
twelve different meanings in the Maori today. Three of them
are significant to Noah:

1. God of Rainbows
2. Island - seen from afar
3. A Raised Place[107]

Noah's three sons were called Shem, Ham, and Japheth
(Genesis 5:32). Nuʻu's three sons were called *Nalu-Akea*,
Nalu-Hoʻohua and *Nalu-Manamana*.[108]

Chapter 4

THE TOWER OF BABEL

There is no known Polynesian account of the Tower of Babel and the scattering of mankind upon the face of the earth. However, Fornander recounts a legend of the Fiji Islands concerning this event.

This account states that in former ages men built a large tower to find knowledge of astronomy. The tower had risen far skyward and the ambitions of the builders seemed near to fulfillment. Suddenly the lower fastenings broke and scattered the workmen over every part of Fiji.[109]

Archaeologist G. Smith found an ancient tablet in the ruins of Babylon that said "*The building of this illustrious tower offended the gods. In a night they threw down what they had built. They scattered them abroad, and made strange their speech.*"[110]

Although the location of this event is different in these accounts, the location of the Fijian account was probably changed over time to a location that Fijians knew.

Chapter 5

GOD'S PLAN IN THE STARS

There is other evidence of the common history of man up to the time of the Tower of Babel. This author believes that there is evidence of an ancient knowledge of the stars and a story that God had put into them. The author also realizes that this is a controversial subject within Christian circles and that there are good people on both sides of this issue. Let the reader decide the truth or fallacy of this issue.

According to Arabic tradition, the ancient knowledge of the stars was handed down by Seth, the son of Adam, and Enoch.[111] Psalm 147:4 says, "*He telleth the number of the stars; he calleth them all by their names.*"

Psalm 19:1-4 says, "*The heavens declare the glory of God; and the firmament sheweth his handiwork. Day unto day uttereth speech, and night unto night sheweth knowledge. There is no speech nor language, where their voice is not heard. Their line* (the ecliptic or the Tabernacle of the Sun) *is gone out through all the earth and their words to the end of the world. In them hath he set a tabernacle for the sun* (the ecliptic, Tabernacle of the Sun)."

The *Tabernacle of the Sun* is the area near the equator within which the sun rises and sets. It was also the boundary at night for all of the constellations which tell the story of God's redemption through Jesus Christ. This boundary is significant because only the constellations within it are visible anywhere on earth! Hence the scripture, *"Their line is gone out through all the earth, and their words to the end of the world."* The Strong's Concordance says that the word *line* in Hebrew, means a cord or rule for measuring.[112]

Job must have known God's story of redemption in the stars because he not only mentions many stars and constellations, but the *Mazzaroth*. Strong's Concordance says that *Mazzaroth* may have meant the *Zodiac* in Hebrew.[113] Nearly 2000 years before the birth of Christ, Job said, *"For I know that my redeemer liveth, and that He shall stand at the latter day upon the earth: and though after my skin worms destroy this body, yet in my flesh shall I see GOD."* (Job 19:25-26). We can still glean from the stars and the constellations of the Zodiac (which have been twisted by astrology into occult meanings), the story of the coming Savior.

The Zodiac or Mazzaroth as it is called in Job 38:32, are the constellations which tell the story of God's redemption through Jesus Christ. The word *Mazzaroth* is mentioned twice in the Bible. In Job 38:32, God challenges Job *"Canst thou bring forth Mazzaroth in his season?"* Mazzaroth literally means the *Separated*, the *Divided* or the *Apportioned*. This name refers to the fact that these signs mark the twelve divisions of the year (months). This again, like the word, *line*, refers to measurment. God is saying to Job, "can you bring forth the months and seasons in succession like I can?"

Anyone who has looked up into the heavens and tried to identify the constellations is quickly disappointed because the stars bear little resemblance to the constellations they are supposed to represent. Yet, when we study the ancient Zodiac charts of peoples from all over the earth, we find that many chart the same twelve constellations with their three associated constellations called *decans*. In many lands these signs have been changed to represent things with occultic meaning, but the charts show the same basic constellations.[114] An explanation for this is that they were known before the dispersion of the peoples at the Tower of Babel.

THE UNIVERSAL STAR CALENDAR

All of these ancient peoples also charted the sky by these twelve signs and their decans. Decan signifies ten, each constellation in the zodiac has three decans representing 10° each or 30° per sign. 30° x 12 signs = 360°. Therefore, this charts the entire circle of the ecliptic. With this chart, days, months, and seasons could be calculated. This "sky chart" was also used by ancient mariners for navigation. Homer wrote *"The stars were sent by Zeus as portents for mariners."*[115] The seasonal path of the sun and the moon were also used for these purposes. This is why God says about the heavenly bodies in Genesis 1:14 *"Let them be for signs and for seasons and for days and years."*

The Hawaiians called their ten day star week, *anahulu*. Three anahulu made up one month and thirty-six anahulu made one year.[116] This again connects the Hawaiians with the Middle East and with the area of Babylon where the oldest

star calendars and Zodiac charts are found. The evidence that
the Zodiac and star calendars of ancient peoples can be traced
to this area validates the truth of the Bible.

There is other evidence to prove this point. In his
book *Star Trek to Hawai'i*, Clyde Hostetter came to possess
a bowl whose patterns were actually an extremely accurate
calendar. This calendar used the moon, planets and stars to
accurately chart months, seasons, years, and even lunar and
solar eclipses. It was even more accurate than our current
system of tracking months and years. He traced the origins of
this calendar to the ancient city of Ur. He also found this
pattern calendar in Sumatra (among the proto-Polynesian
Batak people) and on the pottery of the *Lapita* people, whom
archaeologists now agree were the ancient Polynesians.

There are also sun "clocks" in Polynesia, as there are
in many areas of the world, to tell the time of day, the seasons
and to give directions like a compass.[117]

THE POLYNESIAN CONNECTION

Although many Polynesian constellations show no
similarity to those of the Zodiac, some do. These
constellations and the ways their names can be translated, may
be a remanent of their knowledge of God's story in the stars.
Although the meaning of many of the constellations
have changed, the ancient names and meanings for the stars
that they are composed of are still intact in many languages
today. For instance, the Hebrew name for the star, *Arcturus*,

is `Ayish. This star is located between the constellations of the Virgin and Child and the Crown. `Ayish connotes the *Coming Savior* (Hebrew - `Ayish, root - `ûsh meaning literally to *come to help*).[118] The Hawaiians called the star Arcturus, *Hōkūle'a*, the *Star of Gladness*.

Matthew 2:1-2 speaks about wise men from the east coming to Jerusalem saying, ". . . *Where is he that is born King of the Jews? For we have seen his star in the east, and are come to worship him.*" These ancient eastern wise men probably also knew God's story of the coming redeemer in the stars. They may have seen a new star or heavenly sign within the constellation *Coma* as an ancient tradition states. Another tradition says that Zoroaster, the Persian religious leader, was a student of Daniel in Babylon. He was told by Daniel that a star would appear in the constellation Coma when the One whom it foretold would be born.[119] Coma is one of the decans of Virgo the Virgin, where the story of redemption in the stars begins. This constellation depicts a mother holding a babe. The possible connection between these wise men and the Polynesian people will be shown in a later chapter.

The Southern Cross is one of the decans of Libra. Libra and its decans represent the suffering of the redeemer. The Southern Cross is by far the most visible constellation in the southern sky. Because of the gradual shifting of the skies called the *Precession of the Equinoxes*, the last time this constellation was seen in the Jerusalem skies was around the time of Christ.[120]

The Cross in the heavens was prophetic of how the Savior would be sacrificed. Aben Ezra gave its Hebrew name as, *Adom*, which means the *Cutting Off*, as the angel told

Daniel in 9:26, that the Messiah will be "*cut off, but not for himself. . .*"

As God's story of redemption in the sky became corrupted, the cross became a sacred symbol in the religions of many different peoples like the Egyptians, Persians, Assyrians, Hindus, Chinese, Kamtschatkans, Mexican, Peruvians, Scandinavians, Gauls and Celts.[121] The letter *T* or *Tau* was written in nearly all the ancient alphabets as a cross.

In Tahitian, the Southern Cross is called *Tauhā.*[122] This word has a double meaning, *Tau* means beloved in the Maori but is also the ancient Middle Eastern name for the cross. *Tau* or *Kau* in Hawaiian can also mean *to place in sacrifice. Hā* means spirit or life. Tauhā therefore connotes the *Spirit* or *Life Placed in Sacrifice on the Beloved* Cross.

The ancient Hindus retained a knowledge of the Zodiac. The 3000 to 4000 year old Rig Veda says, "*The actual sacrifice is Prajapati* (The Supreme God) *Himself.*" The Sanskrit scholar, H. Aguilar, translates these verses of the '*Satapathabrahmana* as, "*And indeed, there was no other (victim) meet for sacrifice but that one (Prajapati), and the gods set about offering him up in sacrifice. Wherefore it is with reference to this that Rsi has said: 'The gods offered up the sacrifice with the help of the sacrifice - for with the help of the sacrifice they did offer up him (Prajapati), the sacrifice:- these were the first ordinances, for these laws were instituted first.'* "[123]

Ahuena Taylor, a descendant of the priests of 'Io, said one of the veiled names of 'Io was *Uli.* The Hawaiian authority, Mary Kawena Pukui, said that *'Io-uli* is short for *'Io-i-ke-ao-uli,* meaning *'Io in the obscure heavens.*[124] The

Hawaiian researcher, Emerson, translated an invocation to Uli. Part of this chant says:

> "*Uli, the active, the multiform, offshoot of Iku,*
> *Iku , king of kings in heaven, broken for others.*"[125]

1 Corinthians 11:24 says, "*And when he had given thanks, he brake it (the bread), and said, Take, eat: this is my body, which is broken for you: this do in remembrance of me.*"

Maybe this information is a remnant from the story in the stars, maybe it is a remanent passed down to the Indians and Hawaiians by their ancestor Noah, or maybe the Lord God Almighty just gave them this redemptive analogy. Whatever the case, **Jesus, who was God and the King of Kings in heaven, was sacrificed and broken for us.** It is also a stunning revelation of God's active hand in the lives of these peoples. Revelations 13:8 says, "*And all that dwell upon the earth shall worship him, whose names are not written in the book of life of the Lamb slain from the foundation of the world.*"

Castor and *Pollux*, the two stars that mark the heads of the twins in Gemini, are called *Māhoe-hope* and *Māhoe-mua* in Hawaiian. Their names mean the last and first twin.[126] Castor means *Ruler* or *Judge* and Pollux means *Who Comes to Labor* or *Suffer*. In the Maori, they are called *Taulua*, which means the *Beloved Two*.[127] In Tuamotu, they are called *Tauaro*. *Aro* or *alo* anciently meant the *chief's son*.[128] This name, therefore, connotes the *Chief's Son* (the Ruler or Judge) *Placed in Sacrifice on the Beloved Cross* (He Who Comes to Labor or Suffer).

In the ancient Egyptian Coptic language, Gemini was called *Pi-mahi*, which means the United.[129] Gemini shows that the Ruler and Judge is the same as the One Who Will Come to Suffer. Revelation 1:8 says "*I am Alpha and Omega, the beginning and the ending, saith the Lord . . .* " Tau (*Taw*) is the last letter of the Hebrew alphabet.[130]

The star *Spica* that marks the spike of wheat in Virgo's hand means *The Branch*. In the Hebrew, this star is called *Tsemech*, which also means *The Branch*. It is significant that of the more than twenty Hebrew words for branch in the Old Testament, this is the only one which refers exclusively to Messiah.[131] Jeremiah 23:5-6 proclaims "*Behold, the days come, saith the Lord, that I will raise unto David a righteous Branch, and a King shall reign and prosper, and shall execute judgement and justice in the earth . . . and this is his name whereby he shall be called, The Lord Our Righteousness.*" Zechariah 6:12a says ". . . *Thus speaketh the Lord of hosts, saying Behold the man whose name is the BRANCH.*" Spica, in the Hawaiian, is called *Hikianalia*. One meaning of which is *The Promised Arrival of the Long Desired One*.[132]

In Job 9:9, Job says in referring to God, "*Which maketh Arcturus, Orion, and the Pleiades . . .*" Arcturus, as we have already shown, is Hōkūleʻa in Hawaiian and means the *Star of Gladness*. Orion is one of the decans of Taurus the Bull. Taurus represents the Lord returning in power as ruler and judge. Both the Canaanites and Hebrews called God, *El*. El had the title of *The Mighty One* or *The Bull*.[133] Orion means *Coming Forth as Light*. In the Hebrew, Orion is called, *Chesil*, meaning *A Strong One* or a *Hero*. The Egyptians called him, *Hagat*, which means *This is He Who Triumphs*.[134]

Orion is called *Tautoru* in Maori. Tautoru connotes the *Beloved Sacrifice of the Three* (the Triune God). All of these meanings point to Jesus.

Betelgeuse, the brightest star in Orion means *The Coming of the Branch* and *Alnitak* in his belt means *The Wounded One*. The star *Rigel* in his foot raised to crush *Lepus, The Enemy* (anciently portrayed in Persia and Egypt as a snake[135]), means *The Foot That Crushes* and *Saiph* in his other leg means *Bruised*.[136] Therefore, Orion portrays the prophesy of Genesis 3:15, "*And I will put enmity between thee* (the Serpent) *and the woman* (Eve), *and between thy seed and her seed*; *it* (the woman's seed) *shall bruise thy head* (serpent's) *and thou shalt bruise his heel*." It is significant that the word for man in Samoan, *tagata* (*tangata* in Maori, *kanaka* in Hawaiian), means strike the snake (*ta* - strike and *gata* - snake).[137]

This Biblical prophesy portrays the wounding of the Champion of our Faith, but also His final triumph. In Orion, God placed this prophesy in the stars for all men to see.

THE MAKALI'I

Job 9:9 also mentions the Pleiades. The Polynesians marked the commencement of their seasons by the rising of the Pleiades. The Pleiades are called *Makali'i* in Hawaiian, *Makari'i* in Tahitian and *Matariki* in Maori. The primitive year of the Pleiades was an almost universal prehistoric tradition. It is found among almost all races of mankind in both the northern and southern hemispheres. The rising of the Makali'i during the time of the setting sun marked the beginning of the seasons for the Polynesians. In the ancient Middle East, it began when the Pleiades, or the constellation it was a part of, Taurus the great Bull, was on the meridian at midnight. This takes place in November today, but around 2000 B.C., it would have been late September or early October.[138] Why would there be this universal marking of the new year in the fall? Wouldn't it be logical for people to mark the beginning of the seasons in the spring? The answer is in the stars. Taurus, as mentioned earlier, denotes the Lord returning in power as Judge. This constellation is called *Tau* in most of Polynesia and was also called Tau (the Cross) in ancient Egypt, revealing a possible connection.[139] This bull was probably the now-extinct animal called the *rimu* in Hebrew scriptures. The rimu was a larger and more fierce type of ox than the modern version. It was untamable, and was prized by great hunters and kings. The horns of the bull were its symbol of power and the symbol of horns anciently designated the power and authority of kings and gods.[140] As mentioned previously, one title of the God, *El*, the God of the Canaanites and Hebrews, was the *Bull* or the *Mighty One*. The star that marks the bull's eye is the star, *Aldeberan*. This means the *Governor, Captain* or *Leader*.

The Hawaiian name for the Pleiades, Makali'i, is translated today as "little eyes." This makes "sense" since they are a group of seven small stars. However, in the Maori, it is translated as the *Eye* or the *Appearing of the Chief.* Its spelling should therefore be *Maka-ali'i. Maka* not only means *eye* but can also mean *the source, origin, to begin, start* or *appear.*[141] This connotes the *beginning of the year* or *time of the King.*

The Pleiades were also the eyes of *Viracocha*, the One True God of the Incas.[142] The time of this new year marked by the Pleiades, was looked forward to with great joy and expectation. It represented the coming of something good.

A Maori chant about the new year of the Pleiades says:

Tirohia atu nei, ka whetu rangitia Matariki
Behold, rising brightly, the stars of the Beloved
Great Chief

Te whitu o te tau̲ e whakamoe mai ra
The beloved seven of the new year, the coming
wedding day

He homai ana rongo kia komai atu au
They come with their message of Peace, that I
may rejoice[143]

Revelation 21:9b, speaking of the believers in Jesus Christ, says, *"Come hither, I will shew thee the bride, the Lamb's wife."* When Jesus returns in power on the first day of the seventh epoch of time, he will seek his bride, the church, and usher in a millennium of peace.

This time of year was a time of rejoicing not only because the time of the Beloved King was at hand but also because the time of the enemy of all mankind was at an end. This ending of the enemy's power was represented by the setting of the sign of Scorpio. When the Pleiades and Taurus rise in the sky, the sign of Scorpio, the Scorpion, sets. Scorpio was, in ancient Egypt, represented as a snake. On the Euphrates, it was the symbol of darkness.[144] The Hebrew name for Scorpio is *Akrab*, meaning the *Conflict* or *War*. The Coptic name, *Isidis*, means the *Attack of the Enemy*. The Arabic name is *Al Akrab*, which means *Wounding Him that*

Cometh. The bright red star that marks the heart of the Scorpion is called *Antares*, meaning the *Wounding*.[145] This name shows that Jesus will be wounded by the enemy but He will come forth victorious as shown by Orion.

The ancient Maori name for this star is *Re-hū-ā* (*Ā* - short for atua), meaning the *Hissing God*.[146] Re-hū-ā was a Maori Reptile God and is not to be confused with *Rehua*, the name of a major Maori God and also the name of a constellation.[147] All the seamen of Polynesia still know that this is a *pilau* (foul) star.[148]

The proto-Polynesian *Batak* people of Sumatra represented days with "evil" or "bad" omens with a scorpion. Their name for a scorpion is *hala*.[149] The Hawaiian word for sin is also *hala*.

The Hawaiians celebrated the new year in October with a holy ritual called the *Makahiki*. This is why "Happy New Year" in Hawaiian is *Haoli Makahiki Hou*. This ritual represented the coming of Lono, the God of Peace. In Hawaiian chants, the Pleiades or Makali'i is also associated with the god Lono.[150]

The Hebrews, by specific revelation from God, also observed holy celebrations during October. It started with a ritual announcing the coming year called the *Feast of Trumpets*. This was followed by the *Day of Atonement*. This ritual represented Jesus, the Lord of the Universe, slain as an atonement for the sins of man.

On this day, The High Priest would slay a bull as an atonement of his sins. He would then take the blood of the bull and sprinkle it upon the very mercy seat of God in the Holy of Holies, seven times toward the east (Leviticus 16:6-14).

The Hebrew *Year of Jubilee* also began on the Day of Atonement. This represented the coming time when man would be set free from the bondage of the serpent. The rituals ended with the *Feast of Tabernacles*, also called the *Feast of Ingatherings*. This represented the day when the Lord would return to gather His people and deliver them from this world.

Although this was the first month of the Jewish religious year, it was the seventh month of their calendar year. In this seventh month, on the seventh day of the Feast of Ingatherings, seven bulls were slain in sacrifice. (Numbers 29:32)

Chapter 6

THE POLYNESIANS AND THE ISRAELITES

It is not clear when all the Polynesian people left for the Pacific. It seems that some left at the time of the scattering at the Tower of Babel. The legends indicate that some of them did not separate themselves at this point, but may have been a part of the people who later became the nation of Israel.*

THE POLYNESIAN ABRAHAM

There is very little history available about the time immediately following the tower of Babel in Polynesian as well as Hebrew history.

*The Bible clearly shows that a person is a true Israelite by faith only and not by lineage. Romans 2:28 - 29a says, "For he is not a Jew, which is one outwardly; neither is that circumcision (The act God told the Jews to perform which separated them from other nations and which represented the cutting off of fleshly desires.), which is outward in the flesh: But he is

*a Jew, which is one inwardly; and circumcision is that of the heart, ..."
Therefore, we do not believe that, if the Hawaiian people have some
Hebrew blood in them, they are then made special or gain special favor
with God. We include this section in the book because these legends are a
part of Hawaiian history and not because they are of any particular
significance.*

We are told in each however, about the story of a man
ten generations from Noah (Nuʻu). In Hebrew, this man is
called Abraham.

In the Bible, Abraham is called by God from the
district of Ur in Chaldea, which is at the base of the Uratu
Mountains, to move south into a new country. (The district of
Ur is not to be confused with the city of Ur which was south
of the promised land.)

In Genesis 17:10, he is commanded by God to institute
circumcision as a sign of his covenant with God. In Genesis
16, he sires a son by his slave woman Hagar called Ishmael. In
Genesis 21, he sires another son by Sarah, his wife, called
Isaac. In Genesis 22, Abraham passed a test of obedience to
the Lord because he was willing to sacrifice his son Isaac.

In the Hawaiian tradition, there is a man called
Lua-Nuʻu (*Nuʻu-Lua* in the Samoan[151]), or "the second Nuʻu."
The Hawaiian legends add that he left his native homeland and
moved a great distance until he reached a place called
Honua-ilalo, the *Southern Country*. By the command of his
god, Lua-Nuʻu introduced circumcision to be practiced among
all his descendants. Lua-Nuʻu sired a son by his slave woman,
Ahu, called *Kū-Nawao* (The descendants of Kū-Nawao, the
Nawao people, were called the wild people) and a son,
Kalani-mene-hune, by his chieftess wife *Mee-haku-lani* or
Mee-Hiwa. He is also ordered by his god, Kāne, to go up on
a mountain and perform a sacrifice.[152]

THE POLYNESIAN ISAAC AND HIS SONS

The legend of Kalani-mene-hune corresponds to the story of Isaac in the Bible. He was the progenitor of the *Mene-hune* people and his name could be a description of the promise given to the people who arose from him, *The People of Mene in Heaven.*

Kalani-mene-hune had two sons. The first, and the progenitor of the older branch of the Menehune people, was called *Aholoholo*, the *Wanderer*. The Bible says that the first son of Isaac was called Esau and that he was a hunter and a man of the field (Genesis 25:27).

The second son of Kalani-mene-hune was called *Kini-lau-a-mano*. This name may be a picture of the people who would arise from him; the *Many Descendants of Mano*. He was the father of twelve sons and the original founder of the younger branch of the Mene-hune people. The second son of Isaac was called Jacob. Jacob also had twelve sons and was the progenitor of the twelve tribes of Israel.

The Marquesan legends tell us a similar corresponding story. They say that *Toho* the *Take* (Jacob) was the grandson of *Apana* (Abraham) who introduced circumcision. Toho (Jacob) was the younger of twins born to *I-aaka* (Isaac), the son of Apana (Abraham). Toho had twelve sons and the thirteenth child was a daughter, this is exactly the same as Jacob in the Bible.[153]

THE MENEHUNE PEOPLE

As mentioned previously, Kalani-mene-hune was the progenitor of the Mene-hune people. The Mene-hune (the people of Mene) were the first Polynesian voyagers and settlers of the Pacific Islands. Beckwith says that they were a numerous and powerful race from whom the present race of Hawaiians are descended.[154] This first group of people probably arrived in Hawai'i before A.D. 400 from the Marquesas. They may have been semi-isolated here for 900 years until the next wave of voyagers came from Tahiti.[155]

However, only the first wave of Polynesian peoples called themselves by the name Menehune. This name, although in the genealogies of the latter waves of Polynesian people, was no longer used by these later groups from Tahiti.[156] By this time, Tahiti had been conquered by the next wave of Polynesians that had defeated the Menehune (*Manahune* in Tahitian). Tahiti had been known as *Tahiti Manahune* until it was conquered by this next wave of Polynesians from *Ra'iatea.*[157]*

It has been implied that the Menehune people were made up by the historians Fornander, Kamakau and Kepelino. There is no doubt that they were a real people. A census of Kauai's people taken in the early 1800s recorded 65 people of Menehune ancestry.[158] The Menehune are not only frequently mentioned in Hawaiian and Tahitian history but in those of other Polynesian peoples. Rarotongan traditions state that a group of people named Mana'une accompanied one of their early ancestors from Tahiti. One of the dominant tribes at the time of European contact in Mangaia was the Ngati Mana'une.[159] Lua-Nu'u and Menehune are not only mentioned in the genealogies of the Hawaiians and Tahitians but are also mentioned in the chiefly genealogies of other islands such as Ruanuku.[160]

These first Menehune people were at times defeated and at times assimilated into the later migrations of Polynesian peoples. Being assimilated into the greater number of later peoples, they were no longer called by their old name.

The Menehune were smaller in stature than the later waves of Polynesians. Therefore, as they became a part of the Hawaiian ancestor-'aumakua belief system, the Menehune became the dwarf, quasi-spirit beings that are portrayed today.[161] Buck says that, "*The Menehune pioneers have come to be regarded as gnomes and fairies. It is even said that they were a race of dwarfs, an erroneous description similar to that given by the later story-tellers to their Manahune kinsmen in Tahiti . . .The Menehune were real, live people of Polynesian stock, and they are entitled to the honor and glory of being the first to cross the ocean wastes to Hawai'i.*"[162]

It is a common practice of all warring peoples to characterize their enemies in disparaging terms. This is similar to the American portrayal of the smaller Japanese in World War II posters as grotesque bright yellow dwarfs.

Fornander states that in ancient times, there lived a people called *Minoei* in Southern Arabia. Their capital or chief place was called *Karana*. The similarity of this to the Mene people whose progenitors lived in *Kalana-i-Hauola* cannot be overlooked; especially since the letter "*r*" is "*l*" in Hawaiian! In pre-Islamic Arabia, the prophet or seer was called the *kāhin* or *kāhina*.[163] The Hawaiians called their prophets and seers, *kahuna*. It is also interesting that the sun is called "*la*" in Hawaiian and "*ra*" in most of Polynesia. This is also the terms used for the sun in Egypt and old Babylon.[164]

In an article called *Ethnological Society*, by R. S. Poole, it is also stated that the paintings of the tombs of the kings speak of four races, the first being the ancient Egyptian people called *Men*.[165]

The first historical king of Egypt was also called *Menes* or *Mena*. His tomb has been found at *Abydos*. The dynasty of Menes had nine kings. Some scholars identify him as *Mizraim*, the son of Ham (One of Noah's three sons.). His reign has been dated at between 5500 B.C. and 2000 B.C. by various Egyptologists.[166]

Some researchers report the "Father of the Gods" of the Egyptians was called *Nu*. This is almost identical to the Polynesian Noah's name, Nuʻu! These researchers say that *Nu* and *Nut* (female form of Nu) were the progenitors of the Gods and the founders of the Egyptian civilization. Nu and Nut were two of the *original eight gods* of the Egyptians. These were viewed as gods for having passed through the "judgement" and survived![167] The Bible states that only eight people survived the judgement of the flood.

Menehune could mean the people of Menes. *Hune*, an adjective, anciently signified a collection of people, a class, tribe or nation.[168]

Some of these people of Menes became a part of Israel. At this period in history, there was much mixing between these *Hamite* Egyptians and the *Shemite* Hebrews (Semite — descended from Noah's son Shem). Abraham's slave woman, who bore him Ishmael, was an Egyptian. Joseph, one of Jacob's twelve sons, married an Egyptian. The Hebrew people also lived in Egypt for some 350 years before leaving for the promised land of Canaan (Genesis 16 and 46).

THE POLYNESIAN JOSEPH

Fornander records the Hawaiian legend of *Aukele-nui-a-iku*. He also wrote that this famous legend was known in some form or other on several of the Polynesian groups.[169] This legend is the story of the second youngest of Kalani-mene-hune's twelve children. Aukele-nui-a-iku, being the favorite of his father, was thrown into a pit by his brothers and left to die. He was delivered from this pit by his next eldest brother and then left to succeed in foreign lands. He finally journeyed to the place where the *Ka wai ola-ola a Kāne*, the *Water of Life*, was kept and resuscitated his brothers who had drowned.[170]

The Rev. Sheldon Dibble in his history of the Sandwich Islands, relates the tradition of *Waikele-nui-a-iku* (This name is obviously a tribal variation of Aukele-nui-a-iku). In this account, the hero has ten brothers and one sister. "*Waikelenuiaiku was much beloved by his father but his brothers hated him. His brothers cast him into a pit belonging to Holonaeole. The oldest brother had pity on him and told Holonaeole to take good care of him. Waikelenuiaiku escaped and fled to a country ruled by Kamohoali'i. There he was thrown into a pit under ground in which many persons were confined for various crimes. While confined in this dark place, he told his companions to dream dreams and tell them to him. The following night, four prisoners had dreams. The first dreamed that he saw a ripe 'ōhi'a (apple), and his spirit ate it; the second dreamed that he saw a ripe banana, and his spirit ate it; the third dreamed that he saw a hog, and his spirit ate it; and the fourth dreamed that he saw awa (a Polynesian root), he pressed out the juice, and his spirit drank it. The first three dreams, about food, Waikelenuiaiku interpreted unfavorably, and told the dreamers to prepare to die. The fourth dream, concerning drink, he interpreted to signify deliverance and life. The first three dreamers were slain and the fourth was delivered and saved. Afterward this last dreamer told Kamohoali'i, the king of the land, how wonderful was the skill of Waikelenuiaiku in interpreting dreams. The king then sent and delivered him from prison and made him a principal chief in the kingdom."*

Although these stories are very different in many ways, their similarities to the story of Joseph in Genesis 37-50, cannot be overlooked.

THE POLYNESIAN MOSES

The Hawaiian historians, Kamakau and Kepelino, both relate another ancient legend which has similarities to Biblical history. This story corresponds to the story of Moses leading the Israelites out of Egypt (Exodus 4-5). These two Hawaiian historians apparently received this chant from different sources because they give different details of the story.

In this legend, *Keali'i-Wahanui* (Pharaoh), the king of a country called *Honua-i-lalo* (Egypt), oppressed the *Lahui-Menehune* people (Israelites) in Kamakau's version, and the *Nawao* in Kepelino's version. The God Kāne, sent *Kāne-Apua* (Moses) and his elder brother *Kanaloa* (Aaron) to bring the people away from this evil king.

They were to lead them to the land that Kāne had given them called, *Ka 'Āina Momona-a-Kāne* (The plentiful land of Kāne). In the Bible, this corresponds to Canaan, a bountiful land flowing with milk and honey.

Kāne gave Kāne Apua power and entrusted to him the care of the people. Kāne Apua told Kealiʻi-Waha-Nui (meaning: *The Chief with the Big Mouth*) that Kāne commanded him to let his people go. This chief jeered at Kāne Apua and abused him. This was allowed so that the power of Kāne might be made clear. Lono withdrew rain from the land and there was a famine. Then the chief consented to let the people go.

The people were then told to observe the four *Kū* days in the beginning of the month. These days were *Kapu Hoano*, sacred or holy days. They were to observe these days because they "arose" —*Kū*— and departed from that land.

After leaving the land of Honua-i-lalo, the people came to the *Kai-ʻula-a-Kāne*, the Red Sea of Kāne. There, they were pursued by Ke Aliʻi Wahanui. The people were troubled, wept and were angry with Kāne Apua and Kanaloa. Kāne-Apua prayed to Lono about the trouble because the people were complaining. He said that "*It is an abusive, a wicked people that I am leading.*" Lono commanded him to smite his rod upon the surface of the water and the water parted, exposing the land. The people then went over without trouble, but when chief Wahanui pursued them, he and all his people were drowned.

Kāne-Apua then led his people through desert lands, the people holding on to their wicked ways. When the people became very thirsty, Kāne-Apua thrust his staff at a stone twice and water flowed from it. However, because he thrusted at the stone twice, he did wrong to Lono. In this, Kāne-Apua was irreverent. In the end the people finally reached the *ʻĀina-Lau ʻena-a-Kāne*.[171]

THE POLYNESIAN JONAH

Another interesting legend tells about *Naula-a-Maihea*, the Oʻahu prophet. He left Oʻahu for Kauaʻi, was upset in his canoe, swallowed by a whale, and thrown up alive on the beach of *Wailua*. Although the names are of familiar places in Hawaiʻi, this story has many similarities to the story of Jonah.[172]

The similarities in all of these stories are amazing, especially since the Biblical events took place some thirty-five hundred years ago and are recounted by people on the opposite sides of the earth!*

Together with the rise in popularity of the theory of evolution, there has been in recent years in Hawaiʻi, a movement to discredit the Kumuhonua and other legends that seem to validate the Biblical account of creation. Even Fornander wrote that he was inclined to doubt its (the legend's) genuineness and to consider it as a "paraphrase or adaptation of the Biblical account by some semi-civilized or semi-Christianized Hawaiian, after the discovery of the group by Captain Cook. But a broader and better acquaintance with Hawaiian folklore has shown that, though the details of the legend, as interpreted by the Christian Hawaiian from whom it was received, may possibly in some degree, and unconsciously to him, perhaps, have received a Biblical coloring, yet the main facts of the legend, with the identical names of persons, and places, are referred to more or less distinctly in other legends of undoubted antiquity."[173] Some people even imply that Fornander (who had a Christian background), Kepelino and Kamakau (who were Christians), conspired and made up the Kumuhonua and other legends to validate the Christian faith. Having Christian backgrounds, they did use Biblical terms to describe ancient legends, therefore "coloring" them in a Biblical way. However, the accusation that the basic facts of their legends were made up is doubtful for several reasons:

1. These legends have similar counterparts not only in Polynesia but from every part of the world. The Hawaiian legends could be traced back for generations, and were known to various persons residing on different islands who had no communication with each other. Also, both the narrations and songs were best known by the very oldest of the people; those who never learned to read and whose education and training were under the ancient system. These legends were told to the missionaries by the Hawaiians before the Bible was translated into the Hawaiian tongue and before the Hawaiians knew much of the Bible. The Hawaiian who helped in translating the history of Joseph was amazed by its similarity to their ancient tradition.[174]

2. If Fornander, Kepelino and Kamakau conspired to falsify the accounts, they did a very poor job of it. Their legends differed and each gave different versions of the legends at different times. Their versions probably differed because they were handed down to them differently. As Handy says of the Marquesan sacred chants, "Every tribe had its own rendition of these sacred chants."[175] About the Kumuhonua and Nuʻu legends, Fornander says "so runs the Hawaii legends, but the legends of Oʻahu, Maui and Kauaʻi differ somewhat."[176] Fornander had heard at least four different versions of these legends. Their versions changed because they had heard different versions.

If they were trying to promote Christianity, why didn't they include any legends about Christ or New Testament concepts? After the "Moses" legends, why were there no legends about Joshua and Jericho, Gideon, Samson and Delilah, David and Goliath, Elijah and Jezebel, or the other great stories of the Old Testament? Why would they pick instead a very distorted version of the story of Jonah, an incident that occurred after all of these other great events?

3. Kepelino was a devout Catholic. If he was trying to create a Hawaiian version of Genesis, he would have known that the Nawao do not correspond to the Israelites. He would not have used the Nawao tribe as the Israelites in the "Moses" legend. Also, Kepelino knew that the object of his mentors at the mission was to seek accurate information about the Hawaiian culture. For him to create falsehoods for his Bishop would be a grave sin! The fact that he was a devout Catholic supports the idea that his renditions were accurate and not vice versa.

The reason all three of these men gave for recording Hawaiian history was to preserve accurately the oral history of the Hawaiian people before they were lost to future generations. Why should they want to lie and mislead their people?

Fornander was married to a Hawaiian and appreciated the Hawaiian culture. He wanted to preserve his wife's culture <u>because he saw that the missionaries were replacing the Hawaiian culture with their own!</u>[177] Because of what he was doing, Fornander was for years the "object of virulent hatred by many of the most influential clergy and church leaders in the kingdom."[178] Why then would he want to corrupt Hawaiian legends with the missionary culture?

THE GENEALOGIES OF THE POLYNESIANS

Other similarities between the early Biblical tribes and the Polynesian people are in the genealogies of the Polynesian people.

In Fornander's book, *An Account of the Polynesian Race*, are recorded three different Hawaiian genealogies from different sources. Fornander writes, "*I have three different Hawaiian genealogies, going back, with more or less agreement among themselves, to the first created man.*" These genealogies are very similar to those recorded in Genesis and the book of Matthew. Genealogies like these are prevalent throughout Polynesia. This author personally knows a Hawaiian man and a Hawaiian woman who claim they can trace their family back to Kumuhonua (the first man). He also knows a person who spent time with a Maori who claims the same. *Tomas Watene Rosser*, a Maori from New Zealand who has sailed the South Pacific, states that it is common there for people to know their genealogy back to *Nuku* (Nu'u, the Polynesian Noah).

Fornander says that from ancient times, the three genealogies he lists were considered as equal in authority and independent of each other. He considered them the most accurate of the many he received. The *Kumuhonua* and *Pa'ao* genealogies were of the priests and chiefs of Hawai'i. The *Kumu'uli* genealogy was of the chiefs of Kaua'i and O'ahu. It is interesting that all three record the first man and his three sons, and Nu'u (Noah) and his three sons.

The Kumuhonua and the Pa'ao genealogies both continue to include *Lua Nu'u* who corresponds to Abraham and his two sons, *Kū Nawao* (corresponding to Ishmael) and *Kalani Mene Hune* (corresponding to Isaac). They also include the two sons of Kalani Mene Hune, *Aholoholo* (Esau) and *Kinilau-a-Mano* (Jacob), and Kinilau-a-Mano's twelve sons. These genealogies end with *Papa Nui*, the legendary female progenitor of the Polynesian people. These genealogies are from the later comers to Hawai'i, the people who came from Tahiti.

The genealogy of Kumu'uli includes Nu'u (Noah) but does not include Lua Nu'u (Abraham) or his descendants. This genealogy ends with *Wakea*, the legendary male progenitor of the Hawaiian people.[179]

One could speculate that the Hawaiian people are the joining of two different groups of Proto-Polynesians in the marriage of Papa and Wakea. One line, the line of Wakea, splitting off towards the east at the time of the Tower of Babel, and the other splitting off toward the east sometime after the Israelites entered Canaan.*

It has become important to note here that the Kumulipo genealogy chant, although familiar to Fornander (since he was a close associate and friend of Kalākaua and Lili'uokalani), was not mentioned by him as one of the most accurate genealogies. The Kumulipo seems to speak of evolution and, with the popularity of this theory, the Kumulipo has also gained in popularity. The Kumulipo chant is the most recently composed, and therefore the most fully retained genealogy chant available. According to Lili'uokalani, it was composed in the 1700s by Keaulumoku for the dedication of the high chief Lono-i-ka-makahiki.[180] Although beautifully composed, it is, according to Beckwith, "in its present form is evidently a composite, recast from time to time as intermarriage brought in new branches and a fresh traditional heritage."[181] It displays much of the influence of the Pa'ao gods and religion. In fact the entire ritual of which this chant was a part, was conducted to give the young chief the burning, honoring and prostrating kapus which elevated him to the rank of a god.[182] Kelsy and Pokini Robinson believe that the creation part of the chant (the first seven parts) is not a description of evolution but a symbolic picture of the development of the young chief in the womb. The later parts describe his growth to maturity.[183] The young chief was sometimes referred to as a god because, through the ritual (of which this chant is a part), he was elevated to the rank of a god.[184] Pokini Robinson's interpretation is especially valid because she had not been instructed. Her knowledge came only from her long familiarity with the chant practices of chiefly circles.[185] Handy also described Marquesan chants given at the arrival of a first born heir. His summary of their contents: "The words recapitulate the conception, birth, growth, and so on of the child, linking these with the mythical birth of the gods from the level above and the level below. In subsequent sections the chants refer to the making of ornaments, weapons, and utensils for the child, to his canoe, to his sacred house and to various practices such as bathing, etc. . . . connecting all with mythological references to gods and ancient lands. In parts, various gods are summoned to assist in the rite . . . Throughout, there is mingling of narrative referring to incidents connected with the child, mythological references . . . "[186]

CITIES OF REFUGE

When the Hawaiians arrived in Hawai'i, they created places of refuge called *Pu'uhonua* that were similar to the

Cities of Refuge mentioned in the book of Numbers in the Bible.

The Cities of Refuge of the Israelites and the Places of Refuge of the Polynesians (Places of Refuge are found throughout Polynesia) served the same function. They were places a person could flee to and, whether guilty or innocent, be safe from any harm.

Some other similarities they shared were:

1. The areas of refuge were specifically designated as such.

2. The Cities of Refuge of the Israelites were designated in specific districts and were large enough for a man to live his entire life. Kamakau says that in ancient times, places of refuge were large divisions of land cut out from a district.[187] They corresponded to an *ahupua'a* subdistrict. The ahupua'a was a pie-shaped portion of land that extended from the mountain to the sea. It was large enough and contained all that was necessary for a man to live his entire life.

3. The safety of the refugee extended only to the boundaries of the designated area.

4. The safety of the refugee was guaranteed not by earthly powers but by spiritual powers and authority.

5. In the Hebrew refuge, safety from harm was only extended until the accused person could receive a fair trial by his peers. If he were guilty, he was killed. (Deuteronomy 19:1-13) In Polynesia, there is some evidence that this was also the case.[188]

Chapter 7

THE POLYNESIANS' JOURNEY EAST

TRADITIONS OF THE JOURNEY EAST

According to Hawaiian tradition, the Polynesian people lived many generations after the flood on the east coast of a country called *Ka ʻĀina Kai Melemele-a-Kane*, *The Land* or *Coast of the Yellow* or *Handsome Sea*. This land was to the east of *Kalana-i-Hau-ola*, the place where mankind was created.[189] This may have been somewhere on the coast of the Arabian Sea.

Hostetter may have uncovered the time period when one group began their journey east by calculating the movement of heavenly bodies. He used a phenomenon called the *Precession of the Equinoxes* to do this. The Precession of the Equinoxes is caused by the wobble of the Earth as it spins on its axis. Because of this wobble, the earth's position in its annual orbit around the Sun changes over time. The effect of this phenomenon is that the positions of the stars in the sky also change over time. For example, astrological charts today, which are based on the ancient position of the Zodiacal constellations, are no longer valid. The first point of *Aries*, which was the location of the sun at the time of the Spring Equinox, is now in the constellation of *Pisces*! Astrological charts are now out of sync with the sky by about 41 degrees. By the same token, the timing of the spring rites of the proto-Polynesian *Batak* people of Sumatra (which are based on the position of the stars) are also outdated. The Batak people of Sumatra are the people who used the pattern calendar based on the stars that originated in Ur. This pattern calendar was also probably used by the *Lapita* people who were the ancient Polynesians. These Batak people are now performing their spring rites of the new year in May! Charting the position of the heavenly bodies during the now outdated Sumatran spring rites, Hostetter found that these rites were actually based upon the position of the heavenly bodies during the Spring Equinox of approximately 2400 B.C. over Ur![190] This indicates that these Batak people left Ur shortly after this time. This date is also significant because, according to Biblical genealogies, this is also the approximate time of the dividing of the peoples at the tower of Babel! This evidence indicates that the Batak people migrated east from Ur before Abraham left Ur on his journey south in about 2100 B.C. Therefore, they correspond to the Hawaiians of the Kumu'uli genealogy which includes Nu'u (Noah) but not Lua Nu'u (Abraham) or his descendants.

The people of the Kumuhonua and Pa'ao genealogies left at a later date. Their genealogies continue on through Lua Nu'u and his descendants up until the twelve sons of Kinilau-a-Mano (Jacob). The story of a Jonah-like character, Naula-a-Maihea, is the last of the Hawaiian legends which correspond to the Hebrew. However, there is a large gap in the legends between the Kāne-Apua (Moses) story which occurred around

1450 B.C. and the story of Naula-a-Maihea (Jonah) which occurred around 760 B.C. The absence of any of the great Biblical events that occurred during this 650-year period in any of the Polynesian legends is glaring. Why were great events of Hebrew history like the story of Joshua and the walls of Jericho, Samson and Delilah, and David and Goliath missing? Why was there only the story of Jonah which occurred long after these events? The answer to this problem could be that these Proto-Polynesians (whether they were actually a part of Israel or were a people of the area who adopted the Hebrew genealogies and legends) probably left the Middle East shortly after the time of Moses. They then traveled to their next stop in Irihia (India). Sea trade had been flourishing between the Middle East and India for over a thousand years. Vessels would sail down the Tigris and Euphrates rivers to the Persian Gulf and from there sail along the coast of the Arabian Sea to the Indus River and other trading ports of India. The unusual story of Jonah would surely be told by *Ninevite* traders (*Nineveh* was the city Jonah went to) and could have been picked up by the Proto-Polynesian seamen of Irihia.

Back in the night of time, *Takitumu* Maori traditions say that the Maori race lived far to the west. This former homeland was a mainland region known as *Uru*. Fornander wrote that the Hawaiians had a tradition that they came from *Ulu-nui*.[191] This would be *Uru-nui* in Maori, meaning, the *Great Uru*. Uru is also recorded on the ancient Babylonian tablets in the cuneiform script.[192] This name has been interpreted as Ur of the Chaldees, the same land from which Abraham hailed. The region of Ur may have been named for the mountains that it lies at the foot of, the Ararat Mountains. The Ararat mountains are called the *Uratu* mountains in

Armenian.[193] These are the same mountains that Noah's Ark landed upon. Thus Ur may be considered the motherland of the earth because it is where the repopulation of the earth began.

At a certain period, these Maoris were much harassed by warfare with other peoples in that place. Under a chief named *Puhi-rangirangi*, a number of them migrated southeastward to a hot-climate land called *Irihia*.

Another reason for their move was that the Maoris had heard that Irihia possessed a fine food called *ari*.[194] It is significant that the ancient Sanskrit name for India was *Vrihia*, and that this name can only be pronounced in Maori as *Irihia* or *Wirihia*. The word *ari* is the Dravidian word for rice.[195] Although the legends say that ari was the best food taken on the canoes when they migrated from Irihia, rice was not cultivated in Polynesia. When the old Maoris were asked what *ari* was, they did not know anything about it other than it being a small seed.[196]

In Irihia, there was a mountain of the same name that was a very *tapu* (sacred) place. On this mountain, invocations and ceremonies were made to *'Io the Parentless*, the Supreme Being. There also was the wondrous house of learning called *Hawaiki-rangi* or *Hawaiki-nui*.[197] Hawaiki-nui is also one of the names of the Maori's legendary homeland in other legends.[198]

After a prolonged period in Irihia and many wars with the original inhabitants of the land, a number of Maoris sailed east in search of a new home. The original inhabitants of the land with whom the Maoris had wars may have been the *Harappans*, who were the founders of the Indus Valley civilization. Archeological evidence shows that this civilization came into existence about the time of the Tower of Babel. The Harappans were invaded by the *Arayans* from the northwest.

The *Rig-Veda*, composed about 1500 B.C., tells of the struggles between these Arayan invaders and the prior occupants of the land.[199] The design of the ancient Polynesian sailing canoes closely resembles the vessels attributed to the Harappans. The Harappans are known to have journeyed by sea to an ancient country between the Nile Valley and the Red Sea called, *Cush*.[200] In spite of all the "Hebrew" type legends, Fornander believed that the Polynesians were ancient Cushites. Marco Polo spoke of vessels he saw plying the Indian Sea that were of planking sewn together. Fornander wrote that in olden times the Polynesians possessed *"vessels constructed from planks sewn or stitched together in a substantial manner, pitched and painted, decked over. . ."* The Rev. J. Williams related in the early 1800's that, during his residence at Tahiti, there arrived at Papeete a large canoe from Rurutu of the Austral group (700 miles away). It was planked up and sewed together with a hold twelve feet deep.[201]

Whether the Harappans were also a branch of the Polynesians (their civilization disappeared and no trace of the Harappans has been found) or the Polynesians (Arayans?) learned ship building from them, has not been established. In any case, the Maori tradition says that they sailed east, landing and moving on many times, ever steering toward the rising sun.[202]

The Proto-Polynesians at this time were known as *proto-Malayans*. As these proto-Malayans traveled further and further east, being pushed by a steady invasion of peoples of Mongoloid stock, they left a trail of isolated proto-Polynesian communities along the way. Some of these people are still in the Naga Hills of Assam, the Karen Hills of Burma, the remote Tibetan borders, and the islands of Indonesia.[203]

In the article, *History of Jawa,* Thomas Raffles relates a tradition regarding the manner in which *Jawa* (Java) and the eastern islands were originally populated. This tradition says that the first inhabitants of Jawa came in vessels from the Red Sea. It says that they passed along the coast of India into the Indian Archipelago, which was at that time, connected to the mainland. These islands were since separated from the mainland by some natural cause.[204]

In the genealogies of the Hawaiian people, seven generations from Lua Nu'u (Abraham), was a man called *Hawa-i'i-loa* or *Ke Kowa-i-Hawai'i.* His adventures were most probably a composite of many great Polynesian navigators. In the ancient legends, Hawai'iloa discovered the islands of Hawai'i and Maui. Fornander believes that the islands discovered by Hawa-i'i-loa were actually Java and Sumatra. The legend of Hawa-i'i-loa says that there were only two Hawaiian islands at this time and that Hawa-i'i-loa named the islands after himself (Hawa or Jawa).[205] Marco Polo called the island of Sumatra, *Lesser Java.*[206]

Wakea, the legendary progenitor of the Hawaiian people, may have been the ali'i who led his people away from Java into the Pacific. In Java, there are legends of a prince who left with a thousand followers to escape some type of evil or oppression. He led them to a new home in a better land.[207] Fornander says that the period of Wakea, if counted on the shortest genealogy, corresponds to the commencement of the Malay Empire in the Indian Archipelago. According to Javanese historians, *Tritestra* invaded Java in 76 A.D. and commenced wars on the *Rakshasas,* who were the Proto-Malay, Polynesian ancestors. These wars ended in the subjugation, isolation or expulsion of the Rakshasas throughout the Archipelago.[208] Rakshasas means *Ferocious*

Giants. This is a name the smaller Mongoloid invaders would give to the fierce and physically larger Proto-Polynesians.

Zoologists tell us that the type of pig, dog and fowl found in Polynesia were originally from the Indo-Malayan area. These animals could only have been transported by humans.[209] Botanists agree that all of the important plants in Polynesia, except the sweet potato, also originated in the Indo-Malayan region. These also could only have come with human transport.[210]

How the Polynesians got the sweet potato is a topic of much debate because the sweet potato is indigenous to South America. How could the Polynesians have gotten the sweet potato before the Southeast Asians? They must have sailed to South America or the South Americans must have sailed into Polynesia. Many theories have been put forth on this subject, *Thor Heyerdahl* believes that the Polynesians came from South America because it is much easier sailing west by drifting on the prevailing winds. Recently it has been shown, through intensive scientific study of seasonal wind and current patterns, that a voyage in the opposite direction also is possible.[211] DNA studies done on the ancient remains of Easter Islanders show positively that Easter Islanders are of Polynesian ancestry and not Peruvian or Chilean.[212] However, given the evidence, infrequent contact both ways was probable.

After his *Kon Tiki* expedition, Heyerdahl discovered the proper usage of the South American, *guaras*, center board steering system. The proper uses of this system would allow a balsa wood raft to sail up-wind. This would make possible a round trip by the South Americans. The famous navigator and Inca chronicler Sarmiento de Gamboa wrote in the mid 1500s about the consistent Inca claims that there were inhabited islands far out in the Pacific Ocean. His reports were the instigation for the Mendaña expeditions.

Gamboa records that the Peruvian aborigines knew both the correct direction and distance to what we now know as Easter Island. They even pointed out the characteristics of the only landmark to be found en route. It is documented that on this exploratory expedition, Gamboa, the navigator, and Mendaña, the captain, had an argument about the direction they should sail. Gamboa's Inca directions were subsequently not followed. These directions, however, were later proven accurate.

The Inca legends of *Tupac*, a famous king who sailed into the Pacific with a great fleet, discovered inhabited islands and returned, has some interesting parallels to legends in Mangareva. The researcher, Christian, published the Mangarevan traditions of a chief called *Tupa*, a red man, who came from the east with a fleet of canoes of non-Polynesian type. These canoes were more like rafts. Sir Peter Buck published an old Tiripone manuscript that was written by the son of a Mangarevan chief a few decades after European arrival. This manuscript said that an important visitor to Mangareva was Tupa, who came during the reign of brother kings Tavere and Taroi. Tupa sailed to Mangareva through the south-east passage subsequently named *Te-Ava-nui-o-Tupa* (great channel of Tupa). It also says that he went ashore at the island of *Te Kava*. The manuscript states that Tupa told the Mangarevans about a vast land which contained a large population ruled by powerful kings. The Inca accounts refer to *Ava* island or *Ava-chumbi*, one of two islands visited by Tupac.[213]

It is evident that the Polynesian people crossed the Papua New Guinea and Fijian islands on their way deep into the Pacific. There are still pockets of Polynesian people living in those islands today and also in other islands both in Melanesia and Micronesia. Several branches of the Polynesians may have come through these islands at different times by different routes. The Polynesian legends also tell of wars with dark skinned or black people.[214] Also, the *Yali* of central New Guinea build "Cities of Refuge" like the Polynesians.[215]

From Fiji, anthropological evidence shows that the first large island group to be settled was the Tongan group. This is where these voyagers first became identified as the distinct people we know today as Polynesians.

These first settlers were makers of pottery called *Lapita*. Lapita pottery fragments have been found from Southeast Asia to the Marquesas, showing the ability of these people to move freely over great distances of open ocean. As mentioned earlier, these Lapita people have been traced back through Sumatra to Ur of the Chaldees by Hostetter.

It seems that Fiji was the first island chain that the Lapita people found unoccupied. Up to this point, the Lapita pottery fragments, with their associated tools and ornaments, were not found on the most fertile and desirable islands. This shows that the Lapita people were probably latecomers to these islands and found the more desirable islands occupied by others. However, Lapita sites found on Fiji, Tonga and Samoa, are widespread on the main islands of these chains.

Anthropological evidence shows that the Polynesians traveled from Tonga to Samoa and next to the Marquesas. Here the oldest evidence of settlement in Eastern Polynesia is found. Lapita pottery fragments discovered in the Marquesas were analyzed for their geological content and were found to be made from clay located in only one place, the Rewa delta of Fiji.[216] This confirms the movement of the Polynesians from west to east.

The Marquesas became the hub of Eastern Polynesian settlement. From the Marquesas, the Polynesians traveled to the Society Islands (The author has referred to these islands as *Tahiti*; historically, these islands were known by that name) and Easter Island (*Rapa Nui*). Scientists believe that Hawai'i was settled by the Marquesans some time before A.D. 400. The language of the southern Marquesas is the closest to Hawaiian.[217]

Oral histories of this particular event have become confused by the overlapping of different events over time. Whether a tribe or a family in a few canoes were the first settlers of Hawai'i may never be known. Evidence does suggest, however, that their numbers were small.

Cruel gods that demanded human sacrifice and cannibalism were common in the Marquesas. However, these first Hawaiians had a belief in One Creator God who was benign and did not indulge in human sacrifice or cannibalism. The reason that these people left the Marquesas may have been to remove themselves from these prevalent practices and to keep their religion pure.

Polynesian traditions are full of accounts of voyages to other islands. There are traditions of famous Hawaiian navigators sailing to Tahiti, Samoa, Rarotonga and New Zealand (*Aotearoa*). Tahitian traditions of the Maori canoe, *Tainui*, say that Tainui made several voyages to the *Tuamotu* and Marquesas Groups before leaving for New Zealand. Tahitian traditions also say that the *Matatua* canoe of the Maoris also made a voyage to the Marquesas. Rarotongan and Maori traditions state that the *Takitumu* canoe returned to Rarotonga from New Zealand. However, for some reason that is not known, the evidence shows that this small contingent of people were semi-isolated in Hawai'i for up to 900 years.

Some Maori genealogies seem to trace back to Hawai'i. Maori tradition states that a large wave of voyagers came to New Zealand between A.D. 1300 and A.D. 1350 to settle.[218] It is generally agreed that most, if not all, of the canoes to New Zealand stopped in the Cook Islands (some for generations and others for a short time).[219] However, where the Maoris came from before this time is not clear and greatly disputed. Some of the voyagers of these famous canoes trace their families back to a legendary navigator named *Hema*.

Hema and his sons were famous navigators who, it seems, sailed between the different islands as easily as one would in a modern sailboat today. Hema and his sons are mentioned in legends from Hawai'i, Tahiti, Samoa, the Tuamotus, Rarotonga, and New Zealand. It is disputed where this family actually lived because they or their descendants travelled so widely.

Hema was apparently a chief and priest of 'Io. Ahuena Taylor, a descendant of the priesthood of 'Io, claims Hema as an ancestor. It was passed down to her that " *'Io left Hawai'i when the chieftain Hema departed for New Zealand to live after his feudal warfare with his brother Puna.*" She also said, "*Hema did not worship as his gods the guardians of the sea, fresh water, or mountains; so 'Io loved him and went away with him.*"[220]

The Hawaiian legends say that the priests of the "old religion" in Hawai'i were killed by the invader Pa'ao. However, the tradition of Hema may be another reason why there is only a general and veiled knowledge of 'Io left in Hawai'i.

If Hema or his descendants settled New Zealand, it would also explain why there is much detailed knowledge of 'Io in New Zealand. Kamakau says that Hema was the traditional settler in New Zealand with the Menehune. He tells of how, during the reign of Kuali'i of 'Oahu and later of Kamehameha-nui of Maui, the genealogists got together and established the genealogical lines back Hema.[221] The author has also met several Maori who insist that their ancestors came from Hawai'i.

Given the previous information, the following incident is not so unbelievable. Cleighton Ku'ualohaokalaniakea Eaton recounted that in 1980, a group of Maoris came to Hawai'i from New Zealand. There was a *Tohunga* (Kahuna) in this group who had never been to Hawai'i before but who traced his ancestors to Hawai'i. When he went to Hana, Maui, (Where Hawaiian tradition state Hema lived) he was able to find and identify several sacred sites in the area from the information in his genealogy chant alone.

Beckwith wrote that "*The district of Hana in East Maui is the center of localization in Hawai'i for the lives of the Aikanaka-Laka family (Hema family), and traditional chants are preserved which tell precisely where each of the five was born, where the afterbirth, umbilical cord, and navel string of each were buried, the place of his death and burial, and sometimes other data, together with lists of place names of which it is doubtful whether they name places where the body rested on the way to burial or have some other significance, factual or spiritual.*"[222]

The author believes that with further research, it will be proven that other priests of 'Io left Hawai'i at the time *Pa'ao* was consolidating his power in the Hawaiian islands. Hawaiian oral history says that Pa'ao had the priests of the old religion killed. It makes much sense that these priests and believers in 'Io, being able seamen and having been defeated in war, would set sail rather than face death. This would not be an unusual reason to leave. Maori tradition says that trouble in Hawaiki such as war, the burning of a house of learning (temple) and the slaying of a chief led to the coming of two earlier ancestral canoes.[223]

THE ANTHROPOLOGICAL TRAIL

In anthropology, it is common for people to name a new land after a similar place in their old land. In America, for example, we have *New* England, *New* Hampshire, *New* York and *New* Jersey that are named after places in Great Britain. We also have areas in our cities called *Little* Tokyo, *Little* Italy and China*town*.

Hence, as the Polynesian peoples crossed the Pacific, they left an anthropological trail of familiar names. Hawa - *i 'i* means *Little* Hawa. Fornander said that: Hawai'i leads back to *Hawai'i* of the Society Group, *Hawa'iki* in the Marquesan Islands and New Zealand, *Sawai'i* (Samoa), *Awa'iki* (Rarotonga), *Habai* (Tonga), to *Hawa* or Jawa, to *Sawai* (Ceram, Indonesia), to *Zaba*, an ancient Cushite city in Southern Arabia.

Puna, names of districts on Hawai'i and Kaua'i show an archaeological trail back to *Puna-auia*, a district in Tahiti, to *Puna-he*, a district on Hiwaoa of the Marquesas, to *Puna*, the name of a mountain tribe in the interior of Borneo, to *Poona*, a district in mid-western, India, and Pun, an old Egyptian name for Yemen in South Arabia.[224]

To Fornander's list, can be added that as Hawai'i is *Savai'i* in Samoa, *Hamoa* near Hana, Maui is *Samoa*. The two main islands of Samoa are *Savai* and *Upolu*. On the big island of *Hawai'i* is a place called *Upolu* Point. It is obvious why this point was named Upolu; from the ocean, it has the same sloping landscape as Upolu, Samoa.

HAWA

Fornander also missed a couple of crucial link in his list of places named *Hawa*. Marco Polo wrote of a city in Persia named, *Hawah*. On the map he drew of the area, Hawah was southeast of the district of Ur and due east of Baghdad. In the Maori, Uru also means west-north-west.[225] This is not only the direction of Ur from Hawah but also from India. Hawah was one of three associated cities, the other two he called *Saveh* (*Shaveh* is the Canaanite name for the *Valley of the King* located just outside of Jerusalem.[226]) and *Kashan*. Shaveh and Kashan are still cities in central Iran.[227] Marco Polo claimed that the three kings, the *magi* who knew of God's story in the stars and went to see the child, Jesus, came from these three cities. He says that the magi left from Saveh and that he saw their Sepulchers at Saveh in A.D. 1271). These people being wise in the knowledge of the stars is yet another piece in our puzzle.[228] The other link Fornander missed was an ancient name for India, *Sindhava*.[229]

Tracing the roots of the word *Hawa*, the root word of Hawai'i (meaning little Hawa), we find many places named Hawa or a dialectic equivalent of that name along the route of the Polynesians. These lead back to the middle east as pointed out earlier.

Renan may have given light to the very root of the name itself. He writes that *Hawa* in Aramaic signifies the very breath of life. The mother of life, the first woman, was called

Hawwa; the master of the woman through whom life came therefore being, *Iahwa* (Yahweh).[230] The Theological Wordbook of the Old Testament says that the "eh" sound at the end of *Yahweh* is a late form, probably post-Davidic. The original sound of the Tetragrammaton *YHWH* (Before 900 B.C. no vowels were used in the Hebrew) was more like *Yahwah.*[231] It is significant that the proto-Polynesian, *Karen* people of Burma called their One True God, *Yuah* or *Y'wa*[232] and that the proto-Polynesian *Batak* (Those with the star calendar) and *Dayak* of Sumatra and the people of Pulo Nias (an island off Sumatra) called heaven, *Holi-Yawa.*[233] All of these Proto-Polynesian and Polynesian people used the Yahwah sound for God and not the Yahweh sound. This is evidence that they left the vicinity of Israel before this phonetic change occurred sometime after 900 B.C..

If we follow Renan's theory, this name, *Yahwah,* may have anciently signified "*'Io* or *Yah, the God* or *life-giver of Hawa,*" the first woman. De Vaux says in *The Early History of Israel,* "*It* (the divine name) *is used in the Bible almost always in the long form of Yahweh but, sometimes in poetry and in the liturgical acclamation haleluyah, in the short form of Yah.*"[234] This may be why the holy name is shortened to *Y'ho, Yo,* or *Y'* at the beginning of proper names, such as *Jo*seph; and *Yah* or *Yahu* at the end of names, such as Eli*jah*; but is never shortened as *Hawa.*[235]

If Renan is correct, the holy name is similar to the name of the first woman in Maori lore *'Iowahine,* signifying, "*the woman of 'Io.*" Renan also believed that the words *Yahwah* and *Eve* were derivatives of the same root word, *Hawa* (pronounced *Havvah*). Eve, in the Aramaic, is Hawa.[236] Therefore, the Moslems call the first woman Hawa. Eve in the Phoenician records is called *Havath.*[237] How *Havvah* came to be pronounced *Eve* is as strange as Yahweh becoming

Jehovah in western dialect! This rendition may have come from the first person of the verb hawa pronounced *ehyeh* or the base for another version of Yahweh spelled *Ieye*.[238]

In the Hebrew, the word hawa, the second part of Yahwah, and the word for Eve are two distinct words. Eve is pronounced with the hard "*h*", *Khawa*. Although *hawa* and *khawa* have been formalized into two different words in the Hebrew, Renan states that "*the distinction between those two articulations scarcely existed before the invention of writing.*" Abraham spoke Chaldee. A precursor to written Hebrew was only beginning around 1400 B.C., some 750 years after Abraham. The word *hawa*, whether written with a soft or hard "*h*", has the same meaning in the Aramaic - *the breath of life*.[239] Also, Eve in the Aramaic and Phoenician is pronounced with the soft "*h*" the same as in Yahwah.

Hawa and *khawa* being formally one root word, Hawa (HWH), would explain why there are some very interesting meanings for *hawa*. The following are some of the meanings of hawa: to live, exist, to be, to breathe[240]; fall, evil desire, ruin, calamity, perverse, mischief, iniquity, lust, covet, wickedness, disaster, greedy, crave[241]

Why would part of the holy name of God mean things like evil desire, mischief, greedy, etc.? One explanation would be that *hawa* was formally the same root as *khawa* and these meanings were connected with Eve. When Eve fell, she was no longer only the mother of life but the root of sin and evil in the world. In Hawai'i this change was designated by a change in the actual names of the first man and woman to names with derogatory meanings.

To the Polynesian, Hawa was also many things: it was the ancient motherland or birth place of the people, current and ancient places of living, an ancient sacred house of learning and worship dedicated to the God 'Io, and, according to *The Hawaiian Dictionary*, *hawa* also meant defiled, unclean, filthy, or daubed with excrement.[242]The words *hala* (*hara* in Maori), meaning sin, vice, offense, fault, or error; *hewa*, meaning mistake, fault, error, sin, blunder, defect, offense, guilt, crime, vice, wrong, incorrect, wicked, sinful, guilty; miss, mismanage, or fail; and *'awa* (*kawa* in most of Polynesia), which is a bitter drink used in religious ceremonies and can also mean bitter or poisonous, are probably also related to *Hawa*.[243]

There are also several references in Maori legends to a god called *Ha*. Ha was another name for 'Io and was sometimes coupled with 'Io. The two names together are *'Ioha*, very similar to the Hebrew, *Yahwa*. The Samoans had a god they called *O-le-Sa*, meaning *The Sacred One*. As mentioned earlier, *"s"* in Samoan is *"h"* elsewhere in Polynesia. One Maori chant speaks of *'Io me Ha* ('Io and Ha) which is similar to the Samoan. In *Niue*, an island east of Tonga, *ha* means *"to be, to exist."* In Samoan, *sa* means forbidden or sacred. In the Maori, *ha* means *"breath or to breathe."*[244] In Hawaiian, *ha* can mean *"breathe or life."*[245] All of these have the same meanings as the Hebrew word *Hawa*. One Maori legend of the first man and woman calls the woman, *'Io-wahine* and the man, *Tiki-au-ha*. Both of these names connote being created by 'Io.[246]

ALOHA

Aloha is also a very interesting word. When broken down to its root words, aloha is:

1. *Alo* - The meaning of many words change over time, to find the following meanings for *alo*, we must go back to the ancient Samoan language (remember, the Hawaiians were also once the ancient Samoans). There were two languages in ancient Samoa, the common language and the *high* (chiefly/priestly) language. In the first Samoan - English dictionary, printed in 1862, *alo* is a chief's child. A chief's child was considered to be divine because the chiefs were considered to be divine.[247] In the sacred *high* language of ancient Samoa, *alo* meant the *son of God*.[248]

2. *Ha* - breath, spirit, or life

Hence, aloha means - the life or the spirit of the divine son of God. This then embodies the three parts of the One True God: the Father, Son and Holy Spirit, the One True God who created all things with his word and breathed life into all living things. To speak the word aloha to someone, then, is to say, "*The spirit of the One True God be with you.*" This explains why aloha is used to greet someone and to say farewell also; it is a blessing. This is the same way the Hebrews use the word, *Shalom*, which means divine peace. To greet someone with "*Shalom*" means, "The *Peace of God be with you.*"

The God of all creation is the embodiment of *Agape* (unconditional) Love. No wonder aloha means love, affection, compassion, mercy, sympathy, pity, kindness, grace, charity and beloved; the One True God is all of these things.

The next time someone greets you with "*Aloha*", think about the blessing that is being poured out upon you.

THE HAWAIIAN ALPHABET

In Hawai'i, a missionary committee was set up to draft the Hawaiian alphabet. They had difficulty deciding on the English letters for several Hawaiian sounds. These sounds were between the sounds represented by English letters or were pronounced differently by different tribes. In order to standardize the phonetics for printing, these missionaries had to decide between the *w* and the *v* sound, the *l* and *r* sound and the *k* and *t* sound. Unfortunately, they seem to have picked the wrong letters. We know that *Hawai'i* actually should be pronounced *Havai'i*. Also, it seems that the *t* should have been picked over the *k*. The *t* sound is used in all of Polynesia except Hawai'i. Most authors of the old diaries and manuscripts on Hawai'i speak of meeting King *Tamehameha* not Kamehameha. The letter *l* is *r* and the letter *w* is *v* in most of Polynesia. If the *v*, *r*, and *t* were picked instead of the *w*, *l* and *k*, Hawaiian would be very close to the Tahitian. The ancient land of the last wave of voyagers to Hawai'i would no longer be called *Kahiki* but *Tahiti*. *Kalo* would also be as it is in Tahiti, *Taro*. The gods *Kū* and *Kāne* would be *Tū* and *Tāne* as it is in most of Polynesia.

As mentioned earlier, some Maoris trace their genealogies to Hawai'i, the *Maori* possibly being the *Kanaka*

Maoli (the old name for the Hawaiian people).[249] As the god *Lono* is *Rongo* in Maori, the *L* sound being changed to an *R* sound, so the Hawaiian, *Maoli*, become *Maori*.

HŌKŪLE'A

    Archaeologists generally believe that the Polynesian peoples moved off into the rest of the Pacific islands from Fiji. However, it was at first believed that these long ocean voyages could only have been accidental. Sophisticated computer simulations have now demonstrated that settlement of the Pacific by random voyaging is statistically impossible.[250]

    How did these people arrive at these islands? The Polynesian people sailed in fragile vessels made of wooden planks that were carved with stone tools, held together with string made from coconut husks and propelled by sails of leaves!

    How these people even reached tiny islands in the middle of the largest ocean in the world was unbelievable to westerners. To think that these primitive people could *accurately navigate* to tiny dots amidst a million square miles of empty blue on blue was simply ridiculous! Even experienced western navigators with maps, sextant and compass could not guarantee a landing. A sailor of Cook's day would therefore say, "*I sail toward Tahiti*," and not "*I sail to Tahiti.*" How could primitive Polynesians, without any navigational equipment, accurately navigate to these islands?

    The fact that these long ocean voyages could regularly be made in double hulled canoes has now been proven by the voyages of the *Hōkūle'a.* Using only the stars, prevailing winds, ocean currents, sea birds and other natural signs, the Hōkūle'a has regularly made landfall in journeys from Hawai'i to Tahiti and back. The voyaging canoe, Hōkūle'a, was named after the star that guides it on its journey back to Hawai'i. In the Polynesian star map, Hawai'i sits directly in line with the star Hōkūle'a. The knowledge of this star was preserved by the ancient navigators.

Possibly inspired into the North Pacific by the prophetic promises of the star Hōkūle'a, the Menehune finally arrived in Hawai'i from the Marquesas sometime before A.D. 400. It was a land of unsurpassed beauty and potential. Today, Hawai'i is still compared to the original Garden of Eden. Soon the skills and industriousness of the settlers, along with the blessings of 'Io, produced an abundance of food for all. The Menehune were secure here with their 'ohana and benign gods for the next 700-900 years. During this time, occasional voyages were made, maintaining contact with the rest of Polynesia.

Sometime between A.D. 1100 and A.D. 1300, voyagers from Tahiti started to arrive and settle on the different islands. The last voyager mentioned in Hawaiian traditions is the priest, *Pa'ao*.

Hōkūleʻa Enroute to Tahiti   Courtesy of Ben Tamura

Hōkūkeʻa - Tautira, Tahiti   Courtesy of Ben Tamura

Chapter 8

THE INVADER PA'AO AND HIS CRUEL FOREIGN GODS

Historically, religions and truths have often been twisted and changed by unscrupulous leaders to gain personal power and control over people. Throughout history, new "*gods*" and new doctrines have popped up — concocted by minds bent on the domination and control of others.

This was no different in Hawai'i.

PA'AO

Although every society has its problems, the evidence shows that the Hawaiians remembered the One Supreme God and worshiped him in relative peace until the priest *Pa'ao* came. Fornander writes of this period that ". . . *the kapus were few and the ceremonials easy; that human*

*sacrifices were not practised, and cannibalism unknown;
and that government was more of a patriarchal than of a
regal nature.*"[251] The historian, Rudy Mitchell, writes that
Pa'ao was a kahuna nui (high priest), ali'i nui (high
royalty), famous navigator and a sorcerer of great power.
He was an ali'i nui of the sacred and powerful royal family
of Ra'iatea. Pa'ao was from Vavau (Bora Bora). In ancient
times, the royal house of Vavau conquered the other islands
of western Tahiti and established themselves at Ra'iatea.
Although this family knew of 'Io[252], they established a new
oppressive religious system with its chief place at
Taputaputea.

This royal family conquered with great numbers of
warriors dedicated to naval tactics. They had a large fleet of
war canoes built for speed and silence. They are said to also
have designed paddles and paddling techniques to be swift
and silent. It was with this technique and their special
canoes that they surprised and conquered the other islands of
western Tahiti. They were given the name *Porapora i te hoe
mamu* (first born of the silent paddle) and *Porapora i te nuu
ta rua* (first born of the fleet that strikes both ways).[253]
Malia Craver was told by her elders that Pa'ao brought
many warrior with him. He probably conquered the
Hawaiian Islands in the same way his family did in Tahiti,
with stealth and skilled warriors.

Most historians estimate that Pa'ao came from
Havai'i around A.D. 1300. He arrived with his warriors,
priests (*kahunas*) and new rulers (*ali'i*). *Havai'i* was the
ancient name of *Ra'iatea* of the Society Group. This group
of islands is more commonly known by the main island of
that group, *Tahiti*. (The author has elected to call these
islands Tahiti in this book.) It seems that the earlier voyagers
from Tahiti integrated more peacefully with the Menehune.

Apparently, there was intermarriage with the Menehune inhabitants and the diminishing of class distinction between the Tahitian ali'i and the commoners.

The legends say that when Pa'ao arrived, he regarded the high chief of Hawai'i, *Kapawa*, a degenerate. The priests and ali'i were not performing the rituals they had formerly performed in Tahiti to retain *mana* (divine power). They did not build the necessary *heiaus* (temples), perform the necessary human sacrifices, or wear the red feather malo (loincloth - the symbol of royalty in Ra'iatea) of kings.

Pa'ao saw islands ripe for conquer. There was no powerful royal house or warriors trained for conquest. He returned to Ra'iatea to bring a new line of ali'i with untainted *mana*. Pa'ao returned to Hawai'i not only with a great many warriors but with the ali'i, *Pili*. Through conquest and intermarriage with the older lines, Pili became powerful in the islands. [254]

Pa'ao, as the high priest of the new royalty also became powerful. To consolidate his power, Pa'ao instituted human sacrifices and changed the Hawaiians' religious rituals. He built the first *luakini* (human sacrifice) *heiau* (temple) on the Big Island (Hawai'i) at *Waha'ula*. [255] Fornander wrote that "*. . . there was a time before that, when human sacrifices were not only not of common occurrence, and an established rule, but were absolutely prohibited. Kapu ke kanaka na Kāne, 'sacred is the man to Kāne'. . .*"[256]

Pa'ao instituted the oppressive *kapu* (tapu or taboo) system and the worship of elemental spirit gods such as *Pele*. Fornander says that Pele worship in Hawai'i is only subsequent to this migratory period. The Pele cult was unknown to the purer faith of the older inhabitants and her name does not even appear in the creation accounts.

Execution of a Kapu Breaker   Courtesy of the Bishop Museum

Pa'ao also changed the benign god, *Kū*, into a vengeful and bloodthirsty god of war.[257] He also brought the *Kanaloa* (Tangaloa) Cult from Tahiti, elevating Kanaloa to a major creation god. The class separation between the Ali'i with their mana and the common Hawaiian again became a huge gulf.

Fornander wrote, "*In the polity of government initiated during this period, and strengthened as ages rolled on, may be noted the hardening and confirming the divisions of society, the exaltation of the nobles and the increase of their prerogatives, the separation and immunity of the priestly order, and the systematic setting down, if not actual debasement, of the commoners, the Maka'ainana.*"[258]

What most people today regard as the religious system of the old Hawaiian people, was not their true religion — **it was a foreign religion introduced by the invader Pa'ao**.

Pa'ao's voyages from Tahiti were the last from other Polynesian islands. The 19th century Tahitian scholar, Teuira Henry, wrote that there formerly was an alliance of Polynesian nations which ended around 600 years ago. This alliance ended because of a dispute at an international meeting of navigators. He said that at the great marae (temple) of Taputapuatea in Raiatea, a Maori was murdered and a curse was put on the marae by one of their priests. Navigators from the different Polynesian nations never met again. By the time Captain Cook arrived, voyaging canoes were only a dim and distant memory.[259]

THE KAPU SYSTEM

The ali'i convinced the common people that they had inherited divine power (mana) and were divinely chosen by the gods to rule. The kapu system was structured around the concept of protecting the *mana*. Complex kapus (laws) had to be kept to keep the mana intact and maintain its balance in nature for the land to be fruitful. Every aspect of Hawaiian life was controlled by strict requirements to maintain the balance and harmony of the mana. While there were many laws that encouraged the wise use of resources,and so forth, the social/political aspects of the kapu system provided an open door for abuse. Although ali'i usually kept the kapus, they did this because the belief in mana and the kapus was what kept them in power. High ali'i were never put to death for breaking kapus, although commoners were sometimes sacrificed to correct the "*imbalance in the mana*" caused by an ali'i's sin.

The Hawaiian people endured much suffering and bondage under this new religious system. The ali'i and kahuna had total power in this system and the common people had no control or say about who came to power. It was very rare indeed for the common people to overthrow an ali'i, and only another ali'i could take his place. Although there were exeptions, the majority of the ali'i and kahunas used their power for personal gain and not for the good of the people.[260] The kapu system was used to keep control and wealth within the select ali'i/kahuna group. Laws strictly controlled every aspect of life.

MANŌ, THE SHARK GOD — ALI'I WOULD SOMETIMES KILL AND CUT THE BODIES OF COMMON HAWAIIANS INTO PIECES, AND FEED THEIR SHARK 'AUMAKUA, OR USED THE FRESH HUMAN MEAT TO ATTRACT SHARKS TO KILL THEM FOR SPORT.

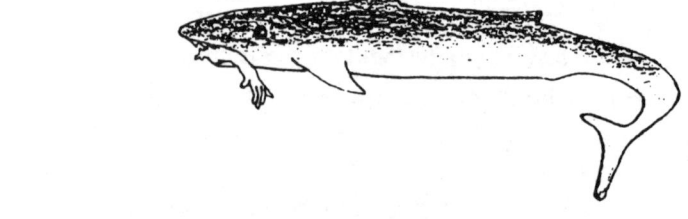

IN THE AREA WHERE FORT ST. MALL IS NOW, A KAHUNA TRAINING HALE WHERE HUMAN HEADS ON POLES LINED THE WALLS.

AT PUNCHBOWL, AN OVEN FOR BURNING HUMANS.

AT KEWALO BASIN, HUMAN VICTIMS WERE DROWNED.

THERE WERE LUAKINI HEIAUS FOR HUMAN SACRIFICE IN VIRTUALLY EVERY DISTRICT OF EVERY ISLAND.

David Kahiapo

For instance, kapus dictated that men and women had to eat separately and were resricted to only certain foods. Common women faced death for eating bananas, coconuts and other foods. Common men also faced death for eating certain fish and other foods. If a commoner stepped on an ali'i's land (even if the boundary was not well marked), or if an ali'i's shadow fell on him, he was also put to death.[261]

An ali'i could take commoners who committed any of these "sins" and use them for human sacrifice or even bait forshark hunting.[262] There were ovens for burning humans at *Punchbowl* and *Waikiki*.[263] Commoners were drowned at *Kewalo Basin (Honolulu)* for breaking kapus.[264] Human heads, of those offered in sacrifice, were put on stakes that lined the *Pakaka* Temple at the foot of Fort Street (Downtown Honolulu).[265] At the heiau located at the foot of Diamond Head, men had their limbs broken with clubs, their eyes scooped out, and then were left bleeding and maimed for three days. They were later clubbed to death with blows to the shoulders rather than to the head, thus prolonging the suffering before death.[266]

The common people owned no land under the new religious system — in fact, they had no rights and <u>nothing</u> they could call their own. An ali'i could take anything he wanted from a commoner: his food, his belongings, his favorite pig, his childern — or even his wife. The ali'i could "tax" most of a commoner's food away and force him to work on his building projects. It is estimated that two-thirds of what the common people produced was taken by high ali'i, chiefs and kahunas. In fact, the common people were so maltreated that when the first anthropologists arrived, they thought that the Hawaiians were comprised of two different races - the huge ali'i and the scrawny common people![267]

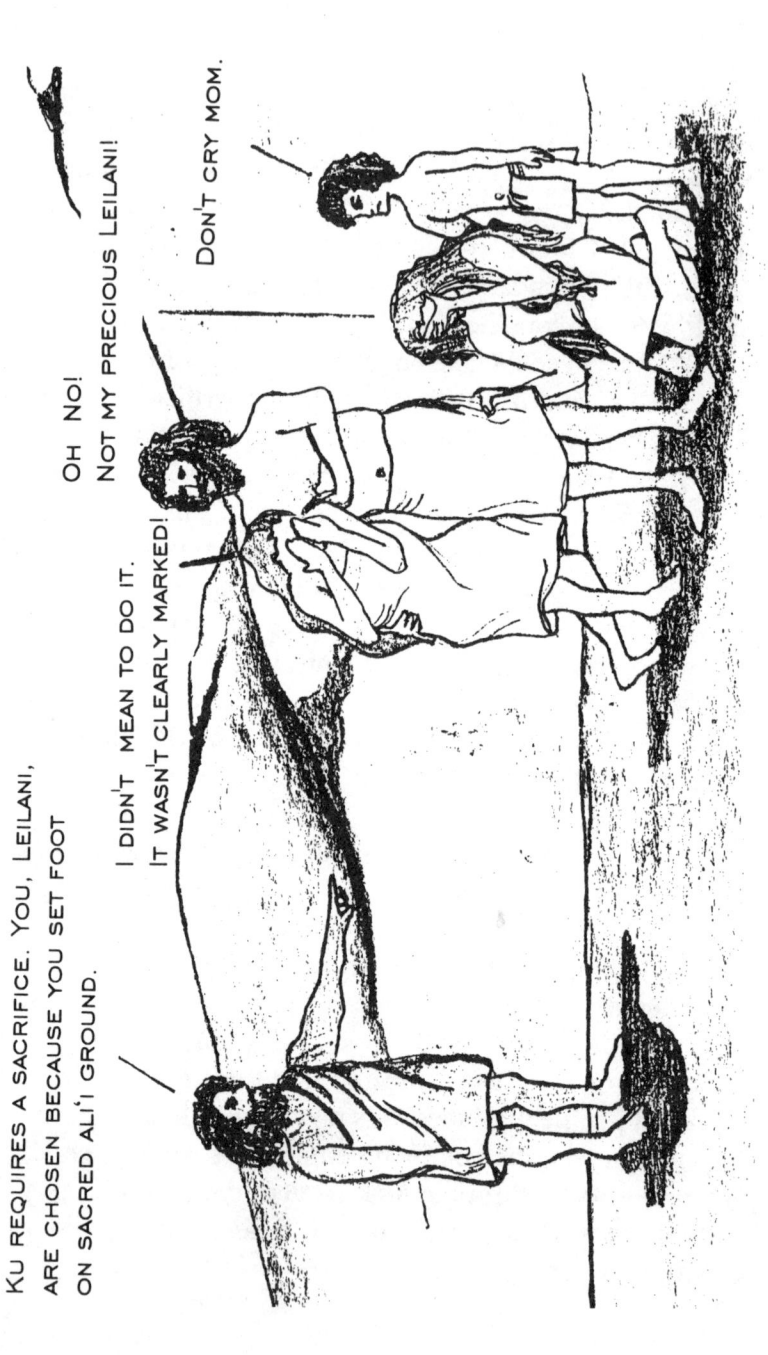

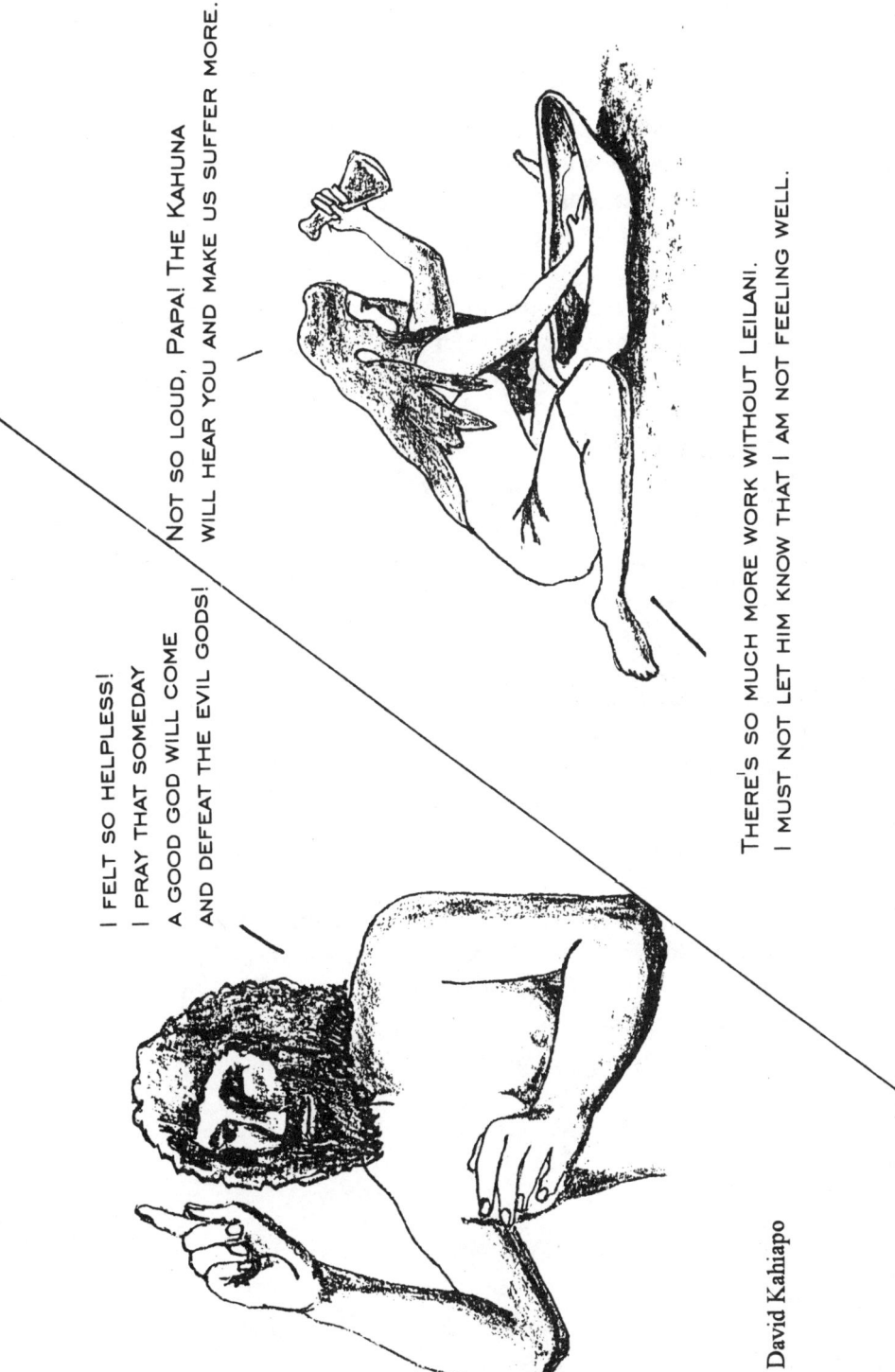

David Kahiapo

Sometimes the kapus were bent to show "mercy", if one could call it that. A five year old girl who ate a banana was treated "mercifully" by the kahunas; they didn't kill her but only scooped out one of her eyes.[268] When the high ali'i, *Kapi'olani*, was a young girl, she ate a banana. Because she was a high ali'i, they did not put her to death. Instead, the kahuna took her favorite servant, a child, and strangled him on the altar of the heiau instead. Many years later, Kapi'olani asked the kahuna who had strangled her young friend why he had done this. The kahuna replied, "*Those were dark days, though we priests knew better all the time.*" The kahuna continued, "*It was power we sought over the minds of the people, to influence and control them.*" Kapi'olani cried out, "*Oh why did not the Christians come sooner and teach us better things!*" She then hid her face in her hands and wept.[269]

One of the most shocking revelations to this author has been that Pa'ao, and his Tahitian kahuna and ali'i, knew about 'Io![270] Considering this, the words which Kapi'olani's kahuna spoke are even more grievous — "*. . . we priests knew better all the time. It was power we sought over the minds of the people, to influence and control them.*"

Even after Western contact, the common people were forced to harvest sandalwood like slaves until their bodies became deformed from carrying the heavy logs. A famine arose when thousands of commoners, forced by the ali'i to harvest sandalwood, could not tend their farms.[271]

Execution of a Kapu Breaker   Courtesy of the Bishop Museum

THE GOD KŪ

Not only were these harsh requirements put on the common people but they were constantly drafted into armies to fight when the aliʻi wanted more power. Captured commoners were used as slaves or for sacrifice. The Hawaiian people were also decimated by these wars. By the time of Kamehameha, there had been some 300 years of nearly constant warfare.[272]

John Young, Kamehameha's trusted foreign advisor, said in 1826 of the conditions he had observed during his forty-nine years in Hawaii, "*I have known thousands of defenseless human beings cruelly massacred in their exterminating wars. I have seen multitudes . . . offered in sacrifice to their idol gods . . .* "[273]

The god Kū, and the new system, had severely oppressed the Hawaiian people.

Through all this oppression, the common people, the *makaʻāinana*, retained great Aloha in their hearts. Their time of freedom from this oppressive system and cruel gods was soon to come.

KAMEHAMEHA

A young warrior named *Kamehameha* rose from the ranks of the aliʻi. He used the technology of the white man to conquer and unify the islands of Hawaiʻi. By unifying the Hawaiian Islands, King Kamehameha played a vital role in the makaʻāinanas' coming freedom from the kapu system.

Chapter 9

THE BONDAGE OF THE CRUEL GODS IS BROKEN

Finally, on October 3, 1819, six months after the death of Kamehameha the Great, the bondage of the kapu system was broken. This day was the first kapu day announcing the coming *Makahiki*,[274] the sacred days of Lono, the God of Peace. Two brave women, wives of Kamehameha the Great, *Ka'ahumanu* and *Ke'opuolani*, and the new king, *Liholiho* (Kamehameha II), openly broke the kapu by eating together at a formal state occasion.

The Hawaiian people were in a state of shock! This was an undeniable public act of defiance. It sent an unmistakable message; the kapu system was no longer honored by the king and the highest ali'i in the land.

These three highest ali'i were supported by Kamehameha's prime minister, *Kalanimoku*, and also the highest kahuna in the land, *Hewahewa*, who was a direct descendant of Pa'ao. Hewahewa was the first one to set torch to a heiau![275]Hewahewa also stated, "*I knew the wooden images of deities, carved by our own hands, could not supply*

*our wants, but worshipped them because it was a custom of
our fathers. . . . My thought has always been, there is one
only great God, dwelling in the heavens.*"[276] Keʻopuolani, the
highest aliʻi in the land said, "*Our gods have done us no good;
they are cruel.*"[277]

Liholiho sent messengers to all the districts of Hawaiʻi
ordering the heiaus desecrated and the images of the gods
overthrown.

Contrary to popular belief, **the missionaries did not
force the Hawaiian people to desecrate their heiaus and
destroy the images of their gods. The Hawaiian people,
following the lead of the aliʻi, rose up and broke the
bondage of that evil system on their own! The overthrow
of the kapu system happened six months before the
missionaries arrived!**

The One True God, whom the Hawaiian people had
worshiped before the coming of Paʻao and the kapu system,
was sovereignly preparing his people to return to Him!

OPUKAHAʻIA

In 1809, ten years before the overthrow of the kapu
system, an orphan from the wars of Kamehameha was offered
passage to the United States by an American sea captain. He
signed on as a crew member of this ship and was given the
English name Henry by the American sea captain. This
orphan's Hawaiian name was *Opukahaʻia*.

OBOOKIAH.

A NATIVE OF OWHYHEE.

Henry Opukaha'ia   Courtesy of the Bishop Museum

Six years earlier, when he was just a boy of ten, Opukaha'ia had seen his mother and father murdered in front of him. As he was trying to flee with his baby brother on his back, a warrior threw a spear at them that killed his baby brother. Opukaha'ia wanted to flee the horrors he experienced in the Hawai'i of his day and to learn about the big and wonderful world beyond the sea.

Even though he was still a boy, Opukaha'ia knew the Hawaiian gods well. He had been apprenticed to his uncle who was the high kahuna of the island of Hawai'i. He had learned the rituals of the kahuna in his uncle's luakini heiau on *Kealakekua Bay*, the same bay Captain Cook had landed at nearly thirty years earlier.[278]

Later, when Henry was introduced to the One True God, he came to realize the absurdity of his old gods. He said, *"Hawai'i gods! They wood, burn. Me go home, put 'em in a fire, burn 'em up. They no see, no hear, no anything. We make them, Our God, (looking up,) **He** make us."*[279] Opukaha'ia accepted Jesus Christ with a glad heart. Opukaha'ia had found the One True God who was kind and merciful, who loved him, and who even sent His son Jesus to die for him.

Eventually ending up in Connecticut, Henry was found weeping on the steps of Yale college because he desired so much to learn. He was taken in by Timothy Dwight, the president of Yale college, and began his western education. Henry's rigorous training for memorizing chants and genealogies at the heiau, turned out to be a blessing in disguise. His sharpened mind learned quickly and the Americans were greatly impressed. Within a few years Henry became quite a scholar, acquiring the equivalent of a Ph.D. degree today.

His great love for God and for his people gave Henry a burning desire to share the Good News of Jesus Christ with his people. He desired to set them free from the oppressive gods and system he had known so well. Henry went to Foreign Mission School to become a missionary to his people. He also traveled throughout New England giving impassioned pleas for churches to send missionaries to Hawai'i.
Opukaha'ia translated the Book of Genesis into Hawaiian directly from the Hebrew. He found that the Hebrew language was similar to his own and, therefore, easier to translate into Hawaiian than the English.[280] He had begun work on Hawaiian grammar, dictionary and spelling books when he fell fatally ill.[281]

Opukaha'ia died praying and weeping for his people, but also with the peace that comes from knowing the abiding love of his God.[282] However, Henry's life was not in vain, God would answer his prayer, his people would hear the gospel of *Iesū Kristo.*

Henry's Memoirs, published in 1819, became the best selling book in New England. It greatly inspired and helped to finance and staff the first Mission Board to native peoples. Up until that time, many people in New England believed that the "heathen" could not be educated and therefore could not accept Christ. By proving to be an exemplary scholar and Christian, this young man shattered both of these misconceptions.

Henry's life not only opened up missions to the Hawaiian people, but to Native Americans and other ethnic groups as well! The first mission to Hawai'i departed Boston in October of 1819; the same time that the Hawaiian people on the other side of the globe were overthrowing their old gods! How wondrously the One True God works!

THE MISSION BEGINS

On October 23, 1819, the day before the Makahiki began[283] and just twenty days after the Hawaiian people broke the bondage of the kapu system, the missionaries set sail from Boston Harbor. With them were four Hawaiians from the mission school. They sailed from the other side of the world, leaving their comfortable homes and pleasant and secure lifestyle. They had given up their pleasant lives and their families to spend five months and 18,000 miles in cramped quarters on the brig *Thaddeus*. They did all this to minister to the Hawaiian people, a people they did not even know.

In late March of 1820, the missionaries arrived. Although full of human faults, all the historians agree that the missionaries had come to Hawai'i with the good of the Hawaiian people in their hearts. Robert Louis Stevenson wrote, *"With all their deficiency of candor, humor, and common sense, the missionaries are the best and most useful whites in the Pacific."*[284] In fact, the Hawaiian people were not so much won over by the teachings of the Love of God or the fear of damnation as they were by the goodness of the missionaries who sacrificed themselves daily to serve the needs of the people.[285]

With a later group of missionaries came another group of Tahitians. This group of Tahitians did not come to rule or to bring death but to serve the Hawaiian people as missionaries of Jesus Christ. Tahitians, being introduced to the gospel of Jesus Christ before the Hawaiians, were brought to help spread the gospel. This was because their language was so similar to Hawaiian. This new group of Tahitians came with the knowledge and power to destroy the evil religion of Pa'ao who had come centuries before them.

Chapter 10

SUPERNATURAL TESTIMONY OF THE ONE TRUE GOD

"God is never without a witness. There is no one who ever lived who can accuse God of not giving them sufficient information to respond to Him. Believing in this has dramatic influence on how we relate to diverse peoples from diverse cultures. We must approach each person with the knowledge that God has been dealing with them and has given them enough information to render all men "without excuse" (Romans 1:18-20). As different people and cultures are studied, the person with a biblical world view will find that God is already there, working."

Mark Beatty
Dean, International College and Graduate School

In the book, *Eternity In Their Hearts*, Don Richardson lists people to whom the One True God left a witness. Starting with the Canaanite, Melchizedek, through the Athenian's unknown god, and on to the experiences of modern day missionaries, he shows that God can, and does speak to peoples other than the Hebrew race.

It was the Hebrew people who kept the "book" intact, and it was the Hebrew people through whom the Messiah, Savior, would come. But Richardson clearly shows that God confirmed to other peoples the Good News of His Son. He lists many incidences of the One True God speaking through a vision or dream to the "holy man" or priest of these peoples.

Many of these holy men were shown that "white men" would bring to them the "book" that would teach them about their One True God. The One True God of the *Gedeo* people of south-central Ethiopia, called *Magano*, showed one of their holy men, in a vision, that two white skinned strangers would erect flimsy shelters under the shade of a large tree near his town. He was told that these men would bring him a message from Magano. Under this very tree, the first missionaries to the Gedeo people set up their tents. This holy man became their first convert and now there are over 200 churches among the Gedeo people.

The proto-Polynesian *Karen* people of Burma also had a revelation. Their revelation was that white foreigners would bring the "book" that their people had lost long ago. This book would bring them back to the true worship of Y'wa (their name for the One True God) and set them free from the "Nats" (demons). The revelation also specified that these white foreigners would come from across the sea in ships with "white wings".

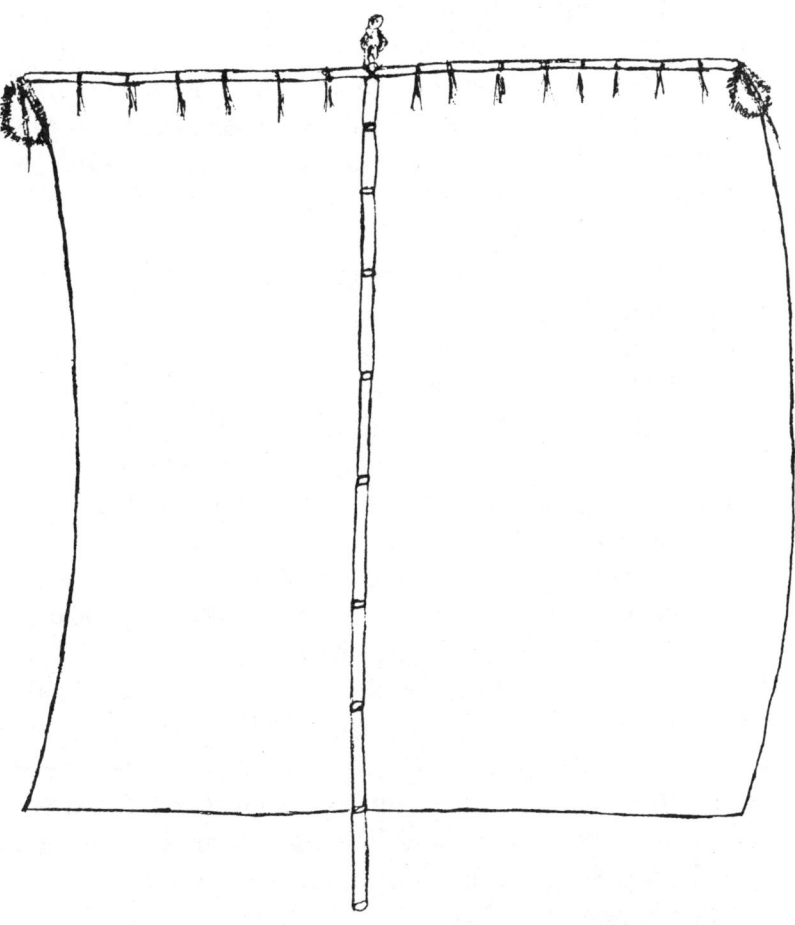

The Makahiki "God"

THE MAKAHIKI SYMBOL

The tradition of the ships with white wings may have been the progenitor of the Hawaiians' symbol for Lono during the Makahiki. The Makahiki heralded the time of Lono, the God of Peace. The Makahiki symbol carried during this time was called *Father Lono* and looked like a square sail. The Polynesians' canoes did not use square sails but triangular sails.

When Captain Cook arrived in the Hawaiian Islands, his ship was resplendent with the symbols of Lono. Cook's ship had sailed around the islands in a clockwise direction, the same direction the symbol of Lono was carried through the islands during the Makahiki. Cook then sailed into *Kealakekua* (short for *Keala ke Akua*, meaning *The Way of God*) Bay, an area considered sacred to Lono. No wonder the Hawaiians believed him to be Lono! They had always expected Lono, the God of Peace, to arrive during the Makahiki season as the stars had foretold. When the Hawaiians eventually realized that Cook was not Lono, he was killed.

Forty years later, after the death of Kamehameha the Great, *Hewahewa*, the highest kahuna in Hawai'i and a direct descendant of Pa'ao, became the first to set torch to a heiau and destroy it. When the old evil system was overthrown on the first kapu day announcing the coming Makahiki, Hewahewa, being the high priest, knew the Prince of Peace was on his way.

Hewahewa knew the prophecy given by *Kalaikuahulu* a generation before. This prophecy said that a communication would be made from Heaven (the residence of *Ke Akua Maoli*, the God of the Hawaiians) by the real God. This communication would be entirely different from anything they had known. The prophecy also said that the kapus of the country would be overthrown.[286] Hewahewa also knew the prophecy of the prophet Kapihe, who announced near the end of Kamehameha's conquests, "*The islands will be united, the kapu of the gods will be brought low, and those of the earth* (the common people) *will be raised up.*" Kamehameha had already unified the islands, therefore, when the kapus were overthrown, Hewahewa knew a communication from God was imminent.[287]

After the overthrow of the kapu system, Hewahewa retired to *Kawaihae,* to wait confidently for the coming of a "*new and greater God.*"

With so many ships with white sails coming to Hawai'i at that time, how would he know which ship would bring the knowledge of the true God of Peace? He could not have known that, although the missionaries set sail on October 23rd, one day before the Makahiki began, they would take six months to arrive. Therefore, it was quite prophetic that, when he saw the missionaries' ship off in the distance, he announced "*The new God is coming.*"[288] One must wonder how Hewahewa knew that this was the ship.

Hewahewa departed for *Kailua* Bay (formally *Kaiakeakua* - Seaside of God) ahead of the missionaries to await their arrival with the King. After Hewahewa's departure, the missionaries' ship entered Kawaihae. Hewahewa's household told the Hawaiians accompanying the missionaries the astounding news that the kapus had been overthrown! The missionaries' ship was then directed to Kailua Bay where the King was in residence.

At Kailua, Hewahewa gave an even more astounding prophecy, he pointed to a rock on the shore and said to the new king, "*O king, here the true God will come.*" When the missionaries arrived at Kailua, they landed their skiff on that very rock! This rock is commonly known as the "Plymouth Rock of Hawai'i."[289]

Hewahewa later retired to *Waimea, O'ahu* and became one of the first members of the church established there. This church is now located in Haleiwa and is called the Lili'uokalani Protestant Church.[290]

Another prophecy was fulfilled by the coming of the missionaries. At the close of one of the symbolic Makahiki ceremonies, as the god Lono was placed in a canoe and sent back to Kahiki, a prophecy was given. The Hawaiians had a tradition that one day the real Lono, of whom this was a symbol, would return. The prophecy was that the Lono god would depart but would return in a small black box. It also said that the people would not know him or recognize the language he spoke. When the missionaries were allowed to land at the "Plymouth Rock of Hawai'i", the first thing they brought ashore was a black bible box. Upon opening the box, no Hawaiian could understand the writing. The Hawaiian priests declared that the prophecy had been fulfilled.[291] Lono, the God of Peace, had finally returned in his new form.

THE FIJIAN GOD OF MANY EYES

The Fijians of Bau, Viti Levu Fiji, had a god of many eyes. The high priest of the idol of many eyes told the ruling chief of Bau that soon a god who could see everywhere would come. Soon thereafter, Christian missionaries arrived fulfilling the prophecy.[292]

THE ATUA OF NEW ZEALAND

When the Christian missionaries arrived in New Zealand, the Maori frequently consulted their gods, the atua (akua), about whether their preaching was the truth or lies. Edward Shortland writes that "*It is a remarkable fact that wherever the inquiry was made, the answer invariably given declared Jesus Christ to be the True God.*"[293]

It is obvious that the One True God communicated to Hewahewa in some way, whether this was by vision, dream, spoken word or conviction, we do not know. However, he definitely knew which ship carried the missionaries and even where they would land. Other Hawaiian priests gave prophecies about the One True God that proved to be true.

As for the Fijian god of many eyes and the Maori atua, the author does not know enough about them to determine if the One True God was speaking to the people through them. These may have been instances of demon gods who could not help but testify of the Lord. James 2:19b says ". . . *the devils also believe, and tremble.*" Demons uncontrollably testifying to the Lordship of Jesus Christ are mentioned in the Bible. In Mark 1:24, a demon says "*Let us alone; what have we to do with thee, thou Jesus of Nazareth? art thou come to destroy us? I know thee who thou art, the Holy One of God.*"

In any case, as it was in many places throughout the world and throughout history, the truth of the Gospel of Jesus Christ was proclaimed in the isles of the Pacific. 'Io, the One True God of the Polynesian people, was allowing it to be known that "*Iesū Kristo (Jesus Christ) is my Son!*" He is the Indian *Prajapati*, the Supreme God who sacrificed Himself.[294] He is the Polynesian *Iku* ('Io), the King of Kings in heaven who was broken for others.[295] He is Jesus Christ, who said, *"this is my body, which is broken for you."* (1 Corinthians 11:24) He is *"the Lamb slain from the foundation of the world."* (Revelations 13:8) He is Jesus Christ, not the Son of the God of the white man, **but the Son of the God of all men**. He is Jesus Christ, not the long awaited Savior of the white man, **but the long awaited Savior of all men**.

Missionary Preaching   Courtesy of the Bishop Museum

Chapter 11

THE GOSPEL COMES

A CHRISTIAN NATION

Although the Hawaiian people heard the Gospel eagerly, progress was relatively slow in the beginning. The missionaries had to first learn the Hawaiian language, create a Hawaiian alphabet (the Hawaiians had no written language), translate the Bible into Hawaiian, and then, letter by letter, set, and finally print the Bible.

The steady, faithful work of the missionaries yielded much fruit in those early years of the mission. However, this progress was soon to be eclipsed.

In 1837, revival broke out. In a few short years, there were more Christians per capita in Hawai'i than in the continental United States! The Kingdom of Hawai'i became known as a Christian nation. The largest church in the world at that time was *Haili* church in *Hilo,* with about 7,000 members.[296] A census taken in 1853 showed a total Hawaiian population of 71,019. Of these, 68,241 claimed membership in a Christian Church, an unbelievable 96%![297] This period, from 1837 to the mid-1850s, was aptly dubbed the *Great Awakening.*

HAWAI'I'S HEROES OF FAITH

There were tremendous Hawaiian heroes of faith during the early years. The change in two of the highest ali'i, *Ke'opuolani* and *Ka'ahumanu* was stunning.

Ke'opuolani was the highest and most sacred ali'i in the land. During the reign of Kamehameha, she had the *fiery kapu*. If Ke'opuolani's shadow fell on any commoner, that person would be thrown into a burning oven.[298] She was considered so sacred that even Kamehameha the Great had to remove his clothing and crawl into her presence.[299] Ke'opuolani had every reason to remain with the kapu system, yet she was one of the first to accept the One True God. She said, "*I have obtained a Savior and a good King, Jesus Christ* (Iesū Kristo)."[300]

Ka'ahumanu, Kamehameha's favorite wife, traveled the country boldly teaching the people about the One True God. She was so changed by Iesū Kristo that many songs were written about the *new* Ka'ahumanu.

Another high ali'i, *Kapi'olani*, defied Pele, the goddess of the volcano, at the active crater of *Kīlauea* - an act of faith and courage so great, it was told around the world in a poem by Tennyson.[301] Kapi'olani said to the people witnessing the event, "*Jehovah is my God. He kindled these fires. I fear not Pele. If I perish by the anger of Pele, then you may fear the power of Pele; but if I trust in Jehovah, and he shall save me from the wrath of Pele when I break through her tabus, then you must fear and serve the Lord Jehovah. All the gods of Hawai'i are vain. Great is the goodness of Jehovah in sending missionaries to turn us from these vanities to the living God and the way of righteousness.*"[302]

Who was this woman of faith? When the missionaries first came to her *hale* (house), Kapi'olani was lying on the floor in a drunken stupor. But after embracing Jesus Christ, this high ali'i began going into the homes of the lowliest commoners, tending to the sick, bringing them food and sewing clothing for them.[303]

There were many other great heroes of faith. *Ulumaheihei Hoapili*, a kahuna of the Order of *Nāhulu*, was Kamehameha's most trusted ali'i. Hoapili was the man whom Kamehameha the Great entrusted to hide his bones after his death. This was the highest mark of trust an ali'i could give to another. Hoapili was also a great warrior and King Liholiho's war leader. When he became a Christian, Hoapili turned Maui into a haven of Christian values.[304]

Hewahewa, the highest kahuna and direct descendant of Pa'ao, was the first to torch a heiau. He later retired to *Kawaihae* to wait confidently for the coming of a "*new and greater God.*" He heard from God because when he saw the missionaries' ship offshore, he announced, "*The new God is coming.*" He also knew the exact spot the missionaries would land. Hewahewa became one of the first members of the Lili'uokalani Protestant Church.[305]

Kalanimoku, the war leader and prime minister of two Kamehamehas, became a Christian. Ali'i such as *Kaumuali'i, Kalakua, Namahana* and *La'anui, Kapule* and *Kaiu, Keali'iahonui* and *Bernice Pauahi* became Christians. Historians *Kepelino, David Malo, Samuel Kamakau* and *John Papa 'Ī'ī* were Christians. *James Kekela, C.M.*

Kamakawiwoʻole, Isaac Iaea, Isaiah Kaʻauwai, L.B. Kaumeheiua, Henry Poepoe, James Kauhane and others became ministers and missionaries to the Pacific.

In the great and ongoing battle between the One True God, ʻIo, and the Great Moʻo (Serpent) for the souls of man, Iesū Kristo had won back a generation of people.

THE MOVING OF THE HOLY SPIRIT

The Hawaiian people have the great distinction of becoming, in a few short years, one of the greatest Christian nations on earth. The revival was so great that it was said, *"One could scarcely go in any direction, in the sugar cane or banana groves without finding children praying and weeping before God."*[306] Families would also rise well before dawn to pray. Titus Coan, the co-pastor of Haili church, wrote that in outdoor meetings, multitudes would be weeping aloud in repentance and prayer.

Meetings were held nightly at Haili Church and people traveled fifty or sixty miles on foot to attend the meetings.[307] Hilo's population swelled from 1,000 people to 10,000, as people hungry for the gospel moved in.[308] Coan sent Hawaiian Christians out two by two to preach the Gospel in Kaʻū and other outlying areas.

Coan also wrote of the generosity of the Hawaiian people. He said that although they were extremely poor, his people did not want to come to church without an offering.[309]

Kapiʻolani Rebukes Pele   Courtesy of the Bishop Museum

THE KING IS IN THE LORD'S HAND

Although the king of the era of the Great Awakening was, at best, a nominal Christian, perhaps the greatest Christian Constitution of any country was granted by him at this time. Proverbs 21:1 says "*The king's heart is in the hand of the Lord, as the rivers of water: he turneth it whithersoever he will.*" What we must remember however, is that the Lord turns his hand in response to his people in prayer. As it was shown in the preceding section, prayers were being lifted up to the Lord for the people and this land as never before nor has been since.

Even a few years before the start of the Great Awakening, much prayer was being lifted up by the missionaries and the Christian Hawaiians. At this time the king, Kamehameha III, was under the influence of alcohol as well as friends and counselors who were totally against Christian values. A day of fasting and prayer was called by the church to petition God specifically for the king.[310] In 1837, revival broke out and the Great Awakening began. As mentioned earlier, great numbers of people began earnestly praying for the people and their country.

On October 8, 1840 (again at the Makahiki season), the king, still a nominal Christian, granted the people of Hawai'i their first Constitution. The Constitution began:

> *God hath made of one blood all nations of men to dwell on the earth, in unity and blessedness. God has also bestowed certain rights alike on all men and all chiefs, and all people of all lands.*
> *These are some of the rights which He has given alike to every man and every chief of correct*

deportment; life, limb, and liberty, freedom from oppression; the earnings of his hands and the productions of his mind, not however to those who act in violation of the laws.

God has also established government, and rule for the purpose of peace; but in making laws for the nation it is by no means proper to enact laws for the protection of the rulers only, without also providing protection for their subjects; neither is it proper to enact laws to enrich the chiefs only, without regard to enriching their subjects also, and hereafter there shall by no means be any laws enacted which are at variance with what is above expressed, neither shall any tax be assessed, nor any service or labor required of any man, in a manner which is at variance with the above sentiments. . . no chief may be able to oppress any subject, but that chiefs and people may enjoy the same protection, under one and the same law.

How different this law was from the laws of the kapu system that had taxed the common people into poverty, used them for slave labor and called for a maka'ainana (commoner) child to be strangled on the altar of a heiau for the sins of the chieftess Kapi'olani! The Constitution continued:

It is our design to regulate our kingdom according to the above principles and thus seek the greatest prosperity both of all the chiefs and all of the people of these Hawaiian Islands. But we are aware that we cannot ourselves alone accomplish such an object - God must be our aid, for it is His province alone to give perfect protection and prosperity. - Wherefore we first present our supplication to HIM, that he will guide us to right measures and sustain us in our work.

It is therefore our fixed decree,

I. That no law shall be enacted which is at variance with the word of the Lord Jehovah or at variance with the general spirit of His word. All laws of the Islands shall be in consistency with the general spirit of God's law.[311]

In 1852, during the waning years of the Great Awakening, a second constitution was passed. This constitution was similar to the first in spirit but went one step further, it changed the government into a Constitutional Monarchy, similar to that of Great Britain. It allowed "*Every male subject of His Majesty, whether native or naturalized, and every denizen of the Kingdom who shall have paid his taxes, who shall have attained the full age of twenty years, and who shall have resided in the Kingdom for one year . . .*" the right to vote.[312]

The prayers of a people seeking God and desiring to do His will, had moved the Lord's hand on a king who was not following God. Hawai'i's laws were some of the most just, fair, and equitable laws on earth.

LAND

Contrary to popular belief, most of the missionaries did not take land for themselves, even though it was offered to them. However, it is true that in later years, land was acquired by some *former* missionaries, those who left their service to Christ and by some children of missionaries.[313]

The true missionaries desired good for the Hawaiian people and tried to prevent their lands from being stolen by wily traders and plantation owners. During the *Great Mahele* (the distribution of land to those other than ali'i), missionaries encouraged the *maka'āinana,* the common Hawaiians, to claim their *kuleanas* (land). They also walked and surveyed the land for them and took them to the land office to help them properly file the legal papers to claim their land.[314] The Rev. John Emerson plotted about eight thousand acres into three hundred lots, nearly every one of these was sold to a native Hawaiian. His parishioners had asked that the land commission appoint him, so that the poor people might obtain their lots without paying a high price for services.[315]

HEALTH

The missionaries also cared for the sick, whether ali'i or maka'āinana (common people). None of the white men who came before the missionaries ever cared about the poor maka'āinana. Ship physicians only served the ali'i to gain their favor. The merchant seamen and men of war had no use for the maka'āinana. There was nothing to gain by treating them.

Missionary doctors, however, had left wealth, prestige and a comfortable life for this life of hardship in a foreign land. They left home for a life of treating the poor for no compensation except for the meager existence of the missionary. This service, however, was rendered with much dedication and love. Their service was not for personal gain, but for a love of God and a desire to spread the love of Jesus Christ to the people they came to serve.

MORALS

Many missionaries were often strict to the point of being harsh. In their zeal to clean out what was evil in the Hawaiian culture, the missionaries often threw out what was good.

For instance, in their zeal to condemn the worship of idols and other false gods, they also condemned some of the art forms such as the hula. The arts themselves are not evil or good, but an avenue of expression. They can be used for good or bad, depending on the focus and intent of the artist. The hula could be used to worship cruel gods, as it was during the kapu system; or it could be used to worship the One True God, 'Io.

In their zeal to control affectionate touching which led to sexual arousal and adultery, the missionaries condemned all touching, except the touching of a husband and wife in seclusion. This also curtailed non-sexual touching as expressions of aloha (love).[316] This "rule" suppressed the very soul of the very affectionate, gregarious and expressive Hawaiian people.

However, the missionaries did not shy away from fighting battles for the good of the Hawaiian people, even if doing so was very unpopular to certain interests. For instance, the missionaries fought against the use of alcohol and gambling, two vices that were the enterprise and downfall of many Hawaiian monarchs. These vices were also extremely destructive to their subjects; many Hawaiians lost their land, their family heirlooms or both in a night of drunken gambling.

The rampant spread of venereal diseases was decimating the Hawaiian people at this time. The missionaries mounted campaigns against prostitution and polygamy that triggered strong protests and even riots from sailors in port. The sailors even tried to lynch several missionaries for this.

Venereal diseases not only increased the mortality rate of the Hawaiian people but also resulted in frequent sterility and miscarriages. The old Hawaiian practice of abortion and infanticide was also opposed by the missionaries.[317] It was estimated that the crude Hawaiian birth rate between 1832 and 1836 was only 25 per 1000.[318]

EDUCATION

From the very beginning, the missionaries taught the Hawaiian aliʻi that the makaʻāinana (common people) possessed "inborn rights." This was a concept that was new to the aliʻi. They also taught them that Christian rulers must look to the welfare of all the people. They told the aliʻi that the huge gap between the poverty-stricken makaʻāinana and the wealthy aliʻi was wrong. Especially since all the labor and goods traded for luxuries were "taxed" from the makaʻāinana, who received none of the benefits.[319]

The missionaries shared with the Hawaiian people whatever skills they possessed to help them increase productivity. They did this to alleviate the poverty of the makaʻāinana. They taught them to dig wells, build with adobe, wood, and coral, construct grinding mills and plow land, among many other things.[320]

One of the main purposes of the missionaries was to teach the Hawaiian people to read and write. This was not only so they could read the Bible, but to prepare them for the wave of white men that was sure to come.[321] At *Lahainaluna* (Maui), the missionaries established the first school west of the Rocky Mountains.[322] The Hawaiian people learned to read so well that 75% of Hawaiians became literate.[323] Hawaiʻi had a higher percentage of literacy than any country in the world![324]

The true missionaries were very concerned about educating the Hawaiian people. They were afraid that the Hawaiians would not be educated enough in the white man's language and ways to survive. Hiram Bingham, the leader of the first group of missionaries, showed his concern when he wrote to the Missionary Board in 1837. He wrote that, unless men with no selfish motives were found to advise the chiefs, *"cunning speculators will ere long . . . give employment to the people as day labor, at a low rate, or introduce foreign labor to their exclusion, and put the products of the soil in their own pocket, thus keeping the aborigines poor, or hastening their extinction."*[325] This prediction, unfortunately, came to pass.

180

Although the Hawaiian people learned to read the white man's language readily, they could not understand the white man's way of money or land ownership until it was too late.

Chapter 12

THE DESECRATION OF THE GOSPEL

"Beware of Te Ma, 'The Unclean One.'
He is always near!"

Chant from the Tainui Maori
House of Sacred Learning

As the true missionaries of Christ returned home, retired in their old age, or passed away, a sinister change began to take place. Over the years, some unscrupulous white traders, planters, and business men, claiming to be Christians, but not following Christ, took up their positions of leadership in the community. Some of these were former missionaries or descendants of missionaries. A distorted understanding of key persons and circumstances and the tendency to compress history over time has caused misconceptions. **The key misconception being that the Christian Church and the** missionaries were responsible for the loss of the Hawaiian Kingdom.

This notion is far from the truth, the true missionaries, left *"without a cent in their pocket*[326]*,"* or died here with nothing. They gave the best part of their lives for the Hawaiian people. Years later, Queen Liliʻuokalani herself would be careful to distinguish between what she called the *"Missionary Party*," made up of unscrupulous "Christians", and the true missionaries to whom she attributed much good.[327]

It must also be understood that, because the United States and Great Britain were considered "Christian Nations," people from these countries were thought to be Christians; even though many were undesireable characters in their own countries! **Most Americans and Englishmen attended church, not because of a deep commitment to Christ, but because it was the accepted and social thing to do.** They attended church because it was traditional and a part of their mores and folkways. Many attended church to be accepted into influencial circles the same way many businessmen play golf or join a prestigious country club today. **These people were not true Christians.**

STANDARD FOR MISSIONARIES

The sponsoring missionary boards required their missionaries to follow specific and explicit rules that **barred them from involvement and interference in the affairs of this world. They were not to take up positions in government or to do any business transactions or take any employment for personal gain. All business transactions** and all employment had to be approved by the other missionaries and all monies earned were to be turned over to the mission. Missionaries could get involved in worldly affairs only if they resigned from the Mission.[328]

For example, the founders of one of the largest companies in Hawai'i, Castle and Cooke, decided to become involved in business and were required to resign from the mission.[329] The missionary doctor, Gerrit Judd, decided to become involved in government and was required to resign from the mission.[330] In other words, missionaries who became involved in worldly affairs, **were no longer missionaries**.

Furthermore, if their motives for involvement in worldly matters were personal wealth and power, **they were no longer followers of Christ!** For Christ said, *"Lay not up for yourselves treasures upon earth, where moth and rust doth corrupt, and where thieves break through and steal: But lay up for yourselves treasures in heaven, where neither moth nor rust doth corrupt, and where thieves do not break through nor steal: for where your treasure is, there will your heart be also . . . No man can serve two masters: for either he will hate the one, and love the other; or else he will hold to the one, and despise the other. Ye cannot serve God and mammon (money)."* (Matthew 6:19-21,24)

The Missionary Board, because of financial problems at home, could no longer support so many missionaries, so it decided to release missionaries to private life. This was done instead of sending them home or elsewhere, in order to keep good strong Christian families in Hawaii.

The Secretary of the Mission Board, however, repeatedly warned the missionaries who retired to private life saying, *"Let me again fraternally warn you not to be `greedy of filthy lucre,' and not to do what may even seem to be taking lands on speculation . . . A sanctified common sense will*

easily draw the line between proper and improper
investments; but let no one trust solely to his own judgement
in such a case. I never yet knew a heart, that I felt sure was
not capable of great self-deception . . . "[331]

The Secretary's words proved to be prophetic. Some
of these former missionaries and their descendants did fall into
self-deception. They fell into thinking that they were doing
what was best for the Hawaiian people; while in reality, they
were doing what was best for their own personal wealth *at the*
expense of the Hawaiian people.

FALSE CHRISTIANS

It is often difficult to know the true character of a
person by how he looks or what label he goes under.
Attending church does not make one a Christian. That is
why the Bible warns that one can only know if a person is a
true follower of Christ or not by the fruit they bear.

As crafty businessmen calling themselves Christians,
but not bearing the fruit of Christ, came into power, so did
greed, pride and self seeking. These are the ones who are
mentioned in 2 Timothy 3:5, who have the outer semblance of
holiness, but not the fruits of Christ. The Bible also warns in
2nd Corinthians 11:13-15, *"For such are false apostles,*
deceitful workers, transforming themselves into the apostles
of Christ. And no marvel; for Satan himself is transformed
into an angel of light. Therefore it is no great thing if his
ministers also be transformed as the ministers of
righteousness; whose end shall be according to their works."

Satan, that evil Mo'o (Serpent) had again enticed man to leave the ways of 'Io, the One True God.

Eventually these businessmen and politicians, some with missionary roots, became the largest landholders in Hawai'i. The companies they built are still the largest landholders today. As of 1987, 38% of the land is owned by the state, 50% by 70 corporations, 10% is owned by the Federal Government, and **less than 1% by small landholders.**[332]

FLAWED MISSIONARIES

If God waited for people to be perfect before He used them, He would not have anyone to use. Although the true missionaries' hearts were right, they were far from perfect. Many of the missionaries condemned the whole Hawaiian culture as pagan and heathen. They failed to see the good qualities in it, for example: the concepts of aloha (agape love – unconditional love), the cities of refuge and ho'oponopono (atoning for wrong and the forgiving of offenses). The missionaries did not realize that this would later become a problem. This automatic rejection of Hawaiian cultural concepts caused confusion, a loss of identity, low self esteem and a subtle resentment in many of their Hawaiian converts. This, in turn, became one of the major underlying causes of the future rebellion of many Hawaiians against Christ. The stage was being set for their return to the gods of Pa'ao.

THE HAWAIIAN PEOPLE RETURN TO
FALSE GODS

The Hawaiian people also became disillusioned with the hypocrisy they saw in many of their white "Christian" brothers. While looking down upon the "uncivilized and heathen Hawaiians," these smug "followers of Christ" were taking advantage of the Hawaiian people to fulfill their greedy and selfish desires.

Tired of "Christian" hypocrisy, and searching for a sense of identity and self worth, many Hawaiians began looking back towards the foreign gods of Pa'ao. They began looking back because they thought they were returning to their true culture. This reverting to the worship of false gods was led by King Lot (Kamehameha V) and later by King Kalākaua.[333] The evil Mo'o was working his devices of deception, greed and selfishness on the ali'i as well as the white foreigners. A return to the kapu system and the gods of Pa'ao meant more power for the ali'i, not the common Hawaiian.

The constitution of 1852 had given universal male suffrage to the common people. This meant that any maka'āinana male could vote. In 1864, King Lot took away universal suffrage, the right of the common people to vote.[334] He said, "*It is clear to me that if universal suffrage is permitted, this government will soon lose its monarchical character.*"[335] This monarch, for his own benefit, denied the right of the common people to decide their country's future. He did this before the *haole* (white) businessmen denied it in 1887. The spirit of greed knows no color or rank.

In 1887, through coercion and veiled threats of assassination, businessmen who controlled the commerce of the nation, forced upon King Kalākaua the "Bayonet

Constitution."[336] This constitution effectively took the power away from the Hawaiian Monarch, and put it more squarely into the hands of these merchants. As with King Lot's Constitution of 1864, the maka'āinana were excluded from any decision-making on the future direction of the country. This was done by requiring a person to own land or meet income requirements in order to vote. These requirements excluded two-thirds of the Hawaiian people from voting, the maka'āinana in particular.[337] One of these businessmen said, "*I have an exalted idea of the destiny of the white man and of his power to control and govern both men and elements.*"[338]

Kalākaua, however, should receive much of the blame for the Bayonet Constitution. King David Kalākaua, the "*Merrie Monarch*," had depleted the kingdom's treasury on his lavish trips abroad, *self*-coronation ceremony, royal luxuries, palace and drinking and gambling parties. He, like other ali'i, mortgaged off Hawaiian lands for loans to support his vices.

Gavan Daws writes of Kalākaua, "*As for David Kalākaua, who came to the throne after Lunalilo, he was a king extravagant in the use of royal prerogatives, sexual, financial, and political, totally improvident, alternately a client and a racial enemy of Americans. His reign was the very negation of missionary teaching. Kalākaua's sister, Lili'uokalani inherited the kingdom only to lose it.*"[339]

During his reign, a *kahu* (pastor), James Kauhane, confronted Kalākaua with a prophesy. He warned Kalākaua that if he did not change his ways, the Hawaiian Kingdom would be lost. Unlike King David of Israel who listened to the words of the prophet Nathan and changed his ways, this King David did not.[340]

A short time later, Kalākaua, while on a royal visit to the United States, died in San Francisco. He was the last king of Hawai'i. Like all the other kings of Hawai'i after Kamehameha the Great, Kalākaua had no son to succeed him. The throne of the Hawaiian Kingdom went to his sister, Lili'uokalani.

Lili'uokalani - Christian Queen   Courtesy of the Bishop Museum

---

Chapter 13

LILI'UOKALANI, THE CHRISTIAN QUEEN

When Lili'uokalani, came to power, she was described as a pious Christian lady by her pastor. She was the organist and choir director of Kawaiaha'o Church. Lili'uokalani would daily spend time praying, reading and meditating on the Word of God. She knew the scriptures well and would lead her household in Bible study daily.[341]

Lili'uokalani tried to rescind the unfair Bayonet Constitution which favored the wealthy and the foreigners over the common Hawaiian. She desired to bring in a new constitution that would restore power to the Monarchy by allowing the common Hawaiian people to vote. When she proposed this, however, she was turned upon by some of the very people who sat in church with her.

THE OVERTHROW

On January 17, 1893, foreign businessmen and landowners, backed by some descendants of missionaries and the United States marines, overthrew the queen. Lili'uokalani refused to allow armed resistance. Seeking to avoid senseless bloodshed and believing that justice would ultimately prevail, she stepped down. She was convicted without receiving a fair trial, and was imprisoned in her own palace.

Many people turned their backs on her. Even her pastor joined in by slandering her. He sent propaganda to the United States to justify the overthrow. He said that she was a pagan and a sorceress who worshiped Pele and sacrificed a pig to pagan gods. Although it is true that Lili'uokalani, like all Christians, was far from perfect, these charges were ridiculous. When Hilo was threatened by Mauna Loa's lava flow, it was Lili'uokalani who asked the churches to open for prayer and led in the prayers. The pig was killed for a birthday luau! In response, Lili'uokalani wrote, "Perhaps I have 'indulged' in harmless 'superstitions' of our native customs in hoping to preserve some of our old traditions. Nevertheless, while the missionaries have ornamented their Christmas trees we have never called them Druids."[342]

Although confused and struggling with what these "Christians" were doing to her, she spent her first night in prison praying. She appealed to the United States, a Christian nation, for justice, and wrote a letter to the Christians of America appealing for help.

Although imprisoned at the hands of Christians and forced to endure their lies, slander and betrayal, Lili'uokalani returned to the Bible again and again for strength in time of need. In prison, she penned *The Queen's Prayer*. Listen to the words of her song:

> *"Your love is in heaven,*
> *and your truth so perfect.*
> *I live in sorrow imprisoned,*
> *you are my light,*
> *your glory my support.*
> *Behold not with malevolence the sins of man*
> *but forgive and cleanse.*
> *And so, O Lord, beneath your wings*
> *be our peace forever more."*

Though imprisoned, her lands and kingdom stolen, her people downtrodden and their cultural identity in shambles, she forgave her tormentors. In the end, the one who was called a pagan and a sorceress by the so-called "Christians," proved to be the True Christian.

Later in life, because of the confused picture of Christianity presented to her by her tormentors, Lili'uokalani searched out a few other religions. The proponents of these religions claimed that their religion better represented her beloved God. In the end, however, she realized that her God was the God of the Bible. This God she recognized in the Bible, however, was not the harsh God of many of the missionaries, but the God she knew and had a personal relationship with. The God who, when she prayed, met her with peace. The One True God she saw in the natural beauty of her islands; the God of the Bible who loved the Hawaiian people.

UA MAU KE EA O KA 'ĀINA I KA PONO

Ua Mau Ke Ea O Ka 'Āina I Ka Pono means *The Life of the Land is Perpetuated in Righteousness*. This legacy, to care for the people and the land in righteousness, was first given by the highest ali'i in the land and the first Christian, Ke'opuolani. On her deathbed, she passed this legacy to her son, the new king, Liholiho (Kamehameha II).[343] Our state motto as we know it today is incomplete. If Ke'opuolani's full legacy is read, it is clear that our state motto should read, "The Life of the Land is Perpetuated by the Righteousness of Iesū Kristo (Jesus Christ)." On her death bed, Ke'opuolani said to her son, the king, "*Take care of these lands which you have received from your father. Exercise a tender care over the people.*" This is where our state motto ends. It has been cut short and is incomplete. Ke'opuolani continued, "***Protect the missionaries, and be kind to them. Walk in the straight path. Keep the Sabbath. Serve God. Love him, and love Jesus Christ.***"[344]

The state motto, in the form that we know it today, was first uttered in 1843 by Ke'opuolani's second son, Kamehameha III. At this time the British had briefly seized control of Hawaii. Upon restoration of the kingdom to him, Kamehameha III gave thanks to God at Kawaiaha'o Church. He also reaffirmed the legacy of Ke'opuolani by speaking the words of the future state motto, Ua mau ke ea o ka ʻāina i ka pono.

The legacy that Queen Liliʻuokalani wanted to leave her people is also clear. She did not want her people to return to demon gods and the kapu system — she wanted to leave her people a *Christian* kingdom. A kingdom that would prevail because it was founded on the eternal truths of the *One True God* and whose people would *perpetuate it by the righteousness of Jesus Christ.*

SUMMARY

The One True God of the Hawaiian people is the same Good God worshipped by all ancient peoples. The Hawaiians are magnificent beings, whose deepest traditions are founded upon the belief that they were created by God in the image of God. The evolutionists' notion that our ancestors were apes has no basis in Polynesian or any ancient culture. As with many other peoples, the progenitors of the ancient Hawaiians, Kumuhonua (Adam) and Keʻolakūhonua (Eve), had a very personal, loving and intimate relationship with their God and Creator. Enticed by the evil Moʻo, the Great Serpent, they sinned (deliberately disobeyed God) and were separated from intimacy with Him. Thus began the continuing battle for the souls of the Hawaiian people from the beginning of time to the present.

The history of Hawaiʻi is a reflection of the history of mankind. From the fall of the first man to the present, there has existed the struggle between good and evil; the struggle for the hearts of man. The first man and woman probably also knew a story told in the stars of a coming Savior, the One who would reconcile man to God. Thus Hōkūleʻa, the star of great joy, is prophetic of Hawaii's identity and destiny.

The human race is an ʻOhana (family), descended from Kumuhonua and Keʻolakūhonua. As descendants, we inherited their character traits—including the tendency to sin against God. The Great Serpent continually enticed man into the worship of false gods. One way or another, all people fell into worshipping false gods who, in time, also took on the identities of ancient heroes or even posed as the One True God Himself. Enticed by the Serpent, new generations of rulers and priests developed sacrificial rituals and complex religious/political systems to gain wealth and to wield power over people. Inevitably, people fell under bondage to these false gods.

Oral tradition indicates that the ancient Hawaiians who discovered and settled Hawaii over 1,600 years ago, knew and worshipped the One True God. However, around A.D. 1300, Tahitian conquerors led by the priest Pa'ao, overthrew the worship of the One True God and established the harsh bondage of the kapu system. Strict order was maintained through horribly repressive laws and the absolute power of the ruling class. Contact with other Polynesians was cut off; the voyaging arts were abandoned. Hawai'i lay in isolation, fear, and oppression for over 500 years.

The coming of the white man, with advanced technology, material resources, and radically different ideologies triggered a social, economic, political, and cultural upheaval. Within months of Kamehameha the Great's death, those he left in charge struck down the malevolent kapu system, and Hawai'i, now in spiritual confusion as well, teetered on the brink of chaos.

Into this scene came the first group of missionaries. They came in response to God's calling through the impassioned pleas of Henry Opukaha'ia. They brought medical aid, education, and services to the downtrodden. But more importantly, they brought the Gospel of Jesus Christ, which struck such a responsive chord that revival broke out in what is now called Hawai'i's Great Awakening. Within a few decades Hawai'i had, per capita, a higher percentage of professing believers than any western nation. The infusion of the Christian faith, with its emphasis on compassion and service, eventually restored peace and order and Hawaii began to prosper.

However, enticed by the Great Serpent, some children of the missionaries, former missionaries and other "Christians" fell into the Serpent's trap of racial pride, greed and power. Hurt and confused by the actions of their "Christian" brothers and following the lead of rulers such as King Lot (Kamehameha V) and King Kalākaua, the Hawaiian people began to slip back into pagan practices. Compounding the problem was the self-indulgent use of resources by Kalākaua which brought the kingdom to the brink of bankruptcy.

In 1887, Kalākaua was forced into signing the *"Bayonet Constitution"* by a clique of American businessmen/landowners. Kalākaua's excesses and incompetence at ruling his kingdom had validated the belief of these businessmen and landowners that they were better fit than the Hawaiians or Orientals to guide the political and economic destiny of Hawai'i.

Queen Lili'uokalani, who succeeded Kalākaua, was a Christian. She had a reputation of caring deeply for her people. In 1892 she sought to introduce a new constitution which would restore to the native Hawaiian some of the rights of citizenship that had been rescinded by the Bayonet Constitution.

The clique of American businessmen/landowners adamantly opposed Lili'uokalani's efforts to include the commoners (non-landowning Hawaiians, and nationalized orientals) in government. The clique formed a conspiracy which, backed by some of the sons of missionaries, marines from an American naval vessel in Honolulu, and an American foreign minister, overthrew the Queen on January 17, 1893.

The Queen refused to allow armed resistance, seeking to avoid senseless bloodshed. She believed that justice would ultimately prevail, and that the kingdom would be restored through diplomatic and judicial processes. But through manipulation, fabrication, and betrayal, the conspirators succeeded in securing their control of this beautiful island kingdom.

Nearly all of the land in Hawaii today is owned by the government. Of private lands, a large portion is still owned or controlled by the companies built by the usurpers, and only 1% by individual owners. Through a long series of malfeasance, deceit, and injustices, many Hawaiians today are not only landless, but also homeless.

Thus, the overthrow of the Hawaiian monarchy is an event that weighs heavily upon the hearts and minds of the Hawaiian people. It is a historic event that has come to symbolize all the hurt, anger, frustration and discontent of the Hawaiian people.

This brings us to a crucial point in Hawaiian history. Will the land be healed and once again be perpetuated in righteousness, or will the land die, and so also die the spirit of the Hawaiian people? Can the people of Hawai'i follow the One True God again? Can the descendants of the overthrowers repent, ask for forgiveness and make right? Can the Hawaiian people repent of bitterness, vengefulness and anger, and forgive? Can the people of these islands again live in brotherhood and aloha?

Time and circumstances may change, but the underlying and overriding issue is repentance and a return to God. 2 Chronicles 7:14 says "*If my people who are called by my name would humble themselves and pray and seek my face and turn from their wicked ways, then I will hear from heaven and forgive their sin and will heal their land."* The healing of hurts, anger, bitterness, injustices and the restoration of a nation can only be accomplished by a sovereign act of God.

It is time for all people of Hawai'i to repent and return to their True Good God through His Son, Iesū Kristo, for *the life of the land is perpetuated by the righteousness of Jesus Christ.*

AFTERWORDS

By Pastor Steve Johnson

Daniel Kikawa

Kahu John Kalili

WHY DID THE REVIVAL END?

By Pastor Steve Johnson

Is it any wonder that the revival died? Haili Church in Hilo had about 7,000 members and often had 10,000 people at services; at a time when the population of Hawai'i could have fit into a large stadium. Today, even with a population of over 1,000,000 people, more than ten times greater than it was at the time of the *Great Awakening*, there is not a church of 7,000 in all Hawai'i.

The Holy Spirit has not worked in mighty power as during the Great Awakening because there is a curse over the land. The curse of injustices, perpetrated in Christ's name, that have not been made right. The prophetic letter Lili'uokalani wrote to the American Christians is coming true in America today.

Lili'uokalani wrote to the Christians of America:

"Oh, honest Americans, as Christians hear me for my downtrodden people! Their form of government is as dear to them as yours is precious to you. Quite as warmly as you love your country, so they love theirs. With all your goodly possessions, covering a territory so immense that there yet

remain parts unexplored, possessing islands that, although new at hand, had to be neutral ground in time of war, do not covet the little vineyard of Naboth's, so far from your shores, lest the punishment of Ahab fall upon you, if not in your day, in that of your children, for "be not deceived, God is not mocked." The people to whom your fathers told of the living God, and taught to call "Father," and whom the sons now seek to despoil and destroy, are crying aloud to Him in their time of trouble; and He will keep His promise, and will listen to the voices of His Hawaiian children lamenting for their homes."³⁴⁵

How great is the love of the Hawaiian people for their God. So many Hawaiians persevere through all the persecution and injustices and hold fast to the Lord. These Christian Hawaiians are great heroes of Faith!

However, many Hawaiians, even Christian Hawaiians, are tormented by hurts, bitterness, despair and vengeful feelings over the injustices they have suffered. Many have not only lost their land, but are now homeless.

THE HEALING OF THE LAND

Now is the time for a healing of this land. The curse over the land must be broken.

It is through God's people that the healing will come. 2 Chronicles 7:14 says, *"If my people who are called by my name would humble themselves and pray and seek my face and turn from their wicked ways, then I will hear from heaven and forgive their sin and will heal their land."*

Hawai'i will again be the Lighthouse of the Lord in the Pacific: if God's people will humble themselves, pray and turn from their wicked ways.

Christians can no longer turn a blind eye and a deaf ear to the theft of the Hawaiian Kingdom by people called by Christ's name. Nor can they ignore the continual stalling of our government to provide restitution or return lands to them. In the Hawaiian Homes program alone (not to mention all the land and monies owed to the Hawaiian people on ceded lands) the Federal-State Task Force on the Hawaiian Homes Commission Act Reported (August 1983) a list of **134 major infractions of the program by the government.** Federally appointed territorial governors had, by executive orders and proclamations, transferred thousands of acres of Hawaiian homestead lands to federal and territorial agencies. Vast tracts of Hawaiian Home lands were also leased at pittances to private sugar and ranching interests.[346] We can no longer ignore the continued suffering of these people who so readily and joyfully accepted Christ and welcomed others to share their islands.

Ironically, there are more Hawaiian and part-Hawaiian families near or below the poverty level today than any other established ethnic group in Hawai'i![347]

Daniel repented and prayed for unfaithful Israel's past sins and God answered by breaking the bondage of Israel's exile in Babylon. We must repent of the injustices done in the islands by our unfaithful Christian ancestors for the curse over this land to be broken.

What better place is there to start than here in the Christian Church, where Lili'uokalani sat side by side with those who betrayed and overthrew her?

LEARN BY PAST MISTAKES

I have a deep admiration and appreciation for the first missionaries to Hawai'i. Their faith and dedication to the Lord and their love and compassion for the Hawaiian people are beyond question. Their lives are a shining example for me. I hope that someday, I may be as Christlike as they were. However, we are all imperfect and make mistakes, and I'm sure that these missionaries would also hope that we learn from their mistakes and not fall into these same mistakes to the detriment of the Gospel.

Because they brought the Good News of Jesus Christ, some missionaries assumed that their culture was also the model Christian lifestyle. The white New England way of living and thinking, however, was not necessarily God's gift to other peoples. In fact, it was probably more different from the culture of the first Christians than the Hawaiian culture was.

Hiram Bingham and his New England group were sure that their strict, unemotional culture was God's design for all people. They were horrified at the Hawaiians exposed flesh and made them wear clothing which was not suitable for the climate. The clothing was also not suitable for working in taro patches, for fishing, or surfing. The missionary style of clothing which covered the human body from head to toe and wrist to wrist, was not only uncomfortable in the Hawaiian heat but down right unhealthy. Dr. Halford believed that the policy of covering the body in clothing would *"increase no end also the incidence of respiratory afflictions due to wetting and evaporation which rendered the enforced use of cotton clothing so much poison to a people whose nakedness had been for centuries a perfect prophylactic.*"[348]

The hula was also completely rejected. Like any art form, the hula takes on the spirit of the god that is worshipped. Long before the arrival of the false goddesses, Laka and Pele, it was probably used to worship the One True God. The Israelites also danced before the One True God. It is about time we take back from Satan what belongs to God! In recent years, this powerful and graceful dance has been reclaimed to glorify God by the hula halaus *Spirit of Joy, Island Breeze* and others.

Some missionaries' belief that their way of life and thinking was holy and right, even restricted the movement of the Holy Spirit! The *Great Awakening* revival started at Titus Coan's and Lorenzo Lyons' churches on the Big Island. As the Holy Spirit swept through the islands, parishioners at Bingham's Kawaiahaʻo church began weeping and falling to the ground in conviction of sin and repentance. Bingham and his group were taken aback by the "*unseemly physical outbursts*" and became critics of the revival even as it was filling their churches! Gavan Daws called Bingham the "Reluctant Revivalist."[349] I point out here that the Israelites also openly displayed their emotions. The emotions displayed by the Hawaiians was at worse, cultural, and at best, the moving of the Holy Spirit.

Affection was also openly displayed in the Hawaiian culture. This was not the case in the New England culture of the missionaries. In fact on the voyage to Hawaiʻi, one of the missionary couples was confronted by the others for practicing the "*most sickening familiarity*" in the cabin and on deck. They were charged with "*holding hands, kissing each other, and openly demonstrating affection in public, thus flagrantly and sinfully corrupting the morals of missionary children and heathen.*"[350]

Kamehameha V recognized that the Hawaiians' sense of self-worth was being lost along with their culture. The Hawaiian people were feeling helpless, useless and defeated.[351] This opened the door for the Hawaiian people to follow him back to the old gods. Some missionaries' inability to see the good in another culture actually served in pushing the Hawaiian people away from Christ.

Let us learn from past mistakes and be open to appreciate and learn from other cultures. Let us follow the example of Titus Coan and Lorenzo Lyons. Titus Coan admired the Aloha of the Hawaiian people and Lorenzo Lyons wrote beautiful hymns and poems in Hawaiian (one of them being *Hawai'i Aloha*). Let us respect cultural mores and folkways instead of trampling upon them and offending those of other cultures.

God gave each people something that reflects His nature. He gave us all something to know Him by, and something to share with other people.

When we come to the Hawaiian people, or *any* people let us come with great humility and great joy. God has allowed us to bring His Good News to His children. Let us come with this gift to give, and also, look expectantly for what gift the Lord has given to the people with whom we share the Gospel.

God has given a gift to each people group so they may know He is there. Romans 1:18-20 says, "*For the wrath of God is revealed from heaven against all ungodliness and unrighteousness of men, who hold the truth in unrighteousness; Because that which may be known of God is manifest in them; for God hath shewed it unto them. For the invisible things of Him from the creation of the world are clearly seen, being understood by the things that are made, even his eternal power and Godhead; so that they are without excuse.*" God has revealed Himself to **all** peoples.

GOD'S GIFT
TO THE HAWAIIAN PEOPLE

by Daniel Kikawa

"ALOHA"

Robert Louis Stevenson wrote to a friend, "*A lovely week among God's best - at least God's sweetest works - Polynesians. It has bettered me greatly.*"[352]

We have much to learn from the Polynesians. The true Polynesian people are also the sweetest people I know. Their Spirit of Aloha can be seen in all of Polynesia. I am not talking about the shallow "*Aloooha!*" yelled out at tourist luaus - this practice is sacrilege to the true Hawaiian! Aloha is the Hawaiian word for God's unconditional love; what the Greek Bible calls *Agape*.
Malia Craver says that if you aloha 'Io, you must aloha everyone.

As mentioned previously, Aloha means literally, *The Spirit of the Son of God*. The Hawaiian Dictionary translates Aloha as: love, affection, compassion, mercy, sympathy, pity, kindness, grace, charity and beloved.

Let me relate a few examples of Aloha:

I once saw a haole tourist admiring a tee shirt a Hawaiian man was wearing. He promptly took the shirt off his back and gave it to the tourist. He refused any money in return.

It is not prudent to go into a real Polynesian home and admire anything, chances are you will be going home with it. Aloha is giving and expecting nothing in return.

I first experienced a real Polynesian home when I was invited to a Hawaiian friend's house. When he introduced me to his mother, a full-blooded Hawaiian, I stuck out my hand and said, "*Glad to meet you Mrs.____.*" She promptly brushed past my hand, gave me a big hug and said, "*Call me Mom! My house is yours, stay as long as you like, and . . . come eat!*"

You will seldom enter a Polynesian home without hearing the words, "*Come eat!*" Aloha is also breaking bread together, not only physically, but spiritually.

Once, my mom bumped into a Hawaiian man's car in a parking lot, denting his fender. He said with a smile, "*Ah, that's okay, only one small dent. The car still work.*" If she had dented someone else's car, chances are we would have had to pay big bucks to fix the dent, or we may have been sued for whatever that person thought he could get out of us! The true Hawaiian knows what is important, not vanity or material things, but relationships. This also is Aloha.

My grandparent's car broke down at night in what was considered a "bad" neighborhood. They walked hesitantly up to a nearby house and asked to borrow the phone. A Samoan family and their friends were having a party there. The Samoans didn't let them borrow the phone. They, instead, went out to the car and found out that the problem was a broken fan belt. They then took the fan belt off their own car and put in on my grandparent's car! From the looks of their home, it was evident that they were not wealthy, but they adamantly refused any money. Aloha is understanding that giving is more blessed than receiving.

"Buffalo" Keaulana, one of the most respected men in the Hawaiian community today, was once asked by an interviewer what makes someone a Hawaiian. He said, "*A Hawaiian is someone who gives and gives and gives until he has nothing.*" A friend of Buffalo's concurred that "*Buffalo had a heart, what he had, he gave it away, even if it left him with nothing.*" If someone gave him something, he would break it up and share it. If, in his job as a lifeguard, he rescued someone and that person sought to reward him, he would say, "*Just thank God and do somebody a favor.*"[353]

The Hawaiian people are also blissfully "color blind." A look at the surnames and the faces of Kamehameha School students makes this statement obvious. All races and racial features are represented there. The true Hawaiian does not look at a person's appearance or skin color, but at his heart!

Some other Hawaiian concepts that Christians can learn from are:

"'OHANA (Family)"

Arline Wainaha Kuuleialoha Eaton teaches her classes that 'ohana is God's gift - "*Ka 'ohana, makana mai ke Akua mai.*"

The *'Ohana* spirit can still be seen today in certain communities.

When my dad had our house built, he worked three jobs to pay for it. He was working so hard we hardly saw him. In contrast, when a Hawaiian friend's father built his house, his friends, family, and neighbors came over to help. While the men worked together, the women cooked together. The children played with their "cousins" (every child there was a cousin). They also learned carpentry, cooking and other skills from mom and dad and aunties and uncles (any adult there was auntie or uncle). When the day was done, they all sat down together to share a meal. There was much "talking story," laughter, music, singing, and dancing.

Both houses got built, but which was built with more loving care? Which built strong family and community ties in the process? This is 'Ohana (family bonding) and Aloha (love and unity in spirit).

'Ohana means respect for the kupuna (elders). The kupuna were respected, cherished and lovingly cared for because of their great wisdom and their sacrifices for the 'ohana.

Mrs. Eaton also says that a strong 'ohana brings lōkahi (balance and harmony). She says that "*The Hawaiian 'ohana is bonded through God's love, God's nature around us and man's caring spirit of aloha."* She also says that the 'ohana is where she learned spiritual principles and how to pray. The 'ohana should be the foundation of a child's spiritual learning. Mrs. Eaton says, *"For I was raised where prayer starts with the 'ohana. The children were taught to memorize a simple Bible verse or **pauku** for 'ohana (family) time. Our 'ohana time would start with mom or dad opening with pule (prayer). Each child would then say their pauku. We would sing some hymns and our kupuna would thank the Lord for the many blessings He had given to us. We would always start and end with a praise and worship song."*

"HANAI"

Hawaiians also do something called *Hanai*. This means that they give one of their children to a friend, relative or neighbor. This friend, relative or neighbor may desire children, but is unable to have children.

Hanai is also done on what is usually a less permanent basis. This is when a friend, relative or neighbor cannot adequately support their child. It may also occur if the parent feels that their child will be better off somewhere else for a while. This may be because of temporary family problems. Whether the hanai is for six months or permanent, the child is immediately accepted as one of the family.

A study of a Hawaiian Homelands community in Leeward O'ahu showed that 30% of the households had children other than their own living in their house.[354] Hanai created a family of the whole community!

From the first day Buffalo Keaulana moved into his house at Makaha, he and his wife opened it up to any and all in need. Three weeks later, they had thirty boys living with them! Any youngster who was an outcast, in trouble or need was welcome. The wife of one man who Buffalo and his wife, Momi, hanai as a child after his parents had died said, "*Thank God she* (Momi) *was there to give Melvin guidance.*"[355]

If all Christians adopted this principle, people would no longer wait long periods of time for children to adopt. People would no longer pay large sums of money to adopt a child. There would be no need for abortion. There would be no orphans and no children who are not cared for properly.

Hanai embodies four principles of Aloha, (1) sacrificing your most precious gift (a child) for the happiness of another, (2) giving of your home and sustenance to help another, (3) accepting and loving strangers as family, and (4) not seeing any of this as a sacrifice!

"HO'OPONOPONO"

The Hawaiians also created a system for handling family or community problems called *ho'oponopono*. E. Shook gives the steps of ho'oponopono as the following:

Ho'oponopono always began with *pule*, a prayer for guidance. The Hawaiian people easily shifted their prayer for guidance to Iesū Kristo, Jesus Christ. This prayer was a foundation for sincerity, truthfulness and humility before God during hoʻoponopono.

Once this foundation was set, the *hala* (transgression) was stated. Hala also meant that both the perpetrator and wronged person were bound together in a relationship of negative entanglements called *hihia*. Hihia could grow into a great tangled knot as the initial hurt and unforgiveness is followed by actions and reactions and more misunderstandings.

The leader picks one of the many tangled problems and slowly untangles the knot through what can be many sessions of hoʻoponopono. As part by part of the knot is untangled, the group can uncover and resolve successive layers of the problem until the relationship is clean.

The leader acts as an intermediary to prevent direct confrontations and further anger and hurt. The emphasis in hoʻoponopono is on self-scrutiny, instead of blaming others. Each person involved, directly or indirectly, is asked to share their *manaʻo,* or feelings. If tempers rise, the leader may call for *hoʻomalu.* This is a cooling off period of silence and prayer to regain the right attitude.

In a Christian setting, the Bible is often opened to gain wisdom on handling the situation.

The next step is *mihi*, the asking of forgiveness and the forgiving. Malia Craver says that mihi is one of the most important steps of hoʻoponopono. In hoʻoponopono, it is expected that forgiveness will be given whenever asked. What needs to be done to right the wrong is also set and agreed upon here.

The participants are also expected to *kala*, loose the negative entanglements and *oki*, cut it off.[356]

Mary Pukui says that such forgiveness extended, "*Mai ka piko o ke poʻo a ka poli o ka wawae, a ma na kihi ʻeha o ke kino.*" From the top of the head to soles of the feet and between all four corners of the body.[357]

Just as God forgives through Jesus, this forgiveness is complete, blotting out the sin like it never happened. One of Liliʻuokalaniʻs favorite scriptures was "*Forgive us our debts as we forgive our debtors.*" She would relate this scripture to hoʻoponopono so her Bible study pupils could understand it better. She would say, "*No one is free from his own sin until he has forgiven him who has sinned against him.*"[358] This coincides with what Malia Craver shared with the author. She said that in order to have *lōkahi* (balance or harmony), we must have mihi in our relationships with all human beings. There must also be *haʻahaʻa* (humility) for there to be lōkahi because without haʻahaʻa, one cannot have mihi.

Hoʻoponopono closes in prayer to thank God for his guidance and forgiveness. They also thank God for the strength and enduring bonds of the group.[359]

Mary Pukui feels that many wars were started because the aliʻi were too proud to submit to hoʻoponopono.[360] With no haʻahaʻa (humility) there was no mihi and therefore no lōkahi.

Hoʻoponopono is not only needed with man but with God and nature. We have much to learn from the Hawaiian kupuna about being in harmony with nature. The destruction and pollution of our environment is now beginning to destroy us.

Arline Eaton tells her students to make a triangle with their hands. This represents the *Triangle of Lōkahi* (balance or harmony). She teaches that this is the Triangle of Lōkahi because harmony can only be achieved when all three sides of the triangle are in balance. At the apex is God, at one bottom corner is man and at the other is the 'aina (the land). **All three are strengthened and founded in Aloha. Aloha is what holds the triangle together. Aloha is the foundation of lōkahi.**

Malia Craver was also taught by her kupuna about the triangle of lōkahi. She was taught that at the apex of the triangle is 'Io (God), on one bottom corner is man and on the other is nature or the 'aina. Malia was taught that **there must be balance between all three for there to be lōkahi.** The triangle is the strongest geometric figure, **but only if all three sides are of equal strength**. Malia says that some Hawaiians today are trying to reach lōkahi with the 'aina, but this cannot be achieved without lōkahi with 'Io. In turn, lōkahi with 'Io cannot be achieved without mihi towards our fellow man, because to aloha 'Io, you must aloha **everyone. All three sides of the triangle are connected, you cannot have lōkahi with one or two sides and not the other. The triangle will be out of balance (lōkahi) and will fall.**

The author would make clear that this does not circumvent the need for restitution of wrongdoing. A makua (parent) can punish and chastise his child in aloha; so also should wrong be made right **with aloha**. As long as a person has aloha for his fellow man, God and nature, that person will retain harmony and peace in his soul, even though those around him do not.

Anger, bitterness, hatred and unforgiveness destroys the lōkahi of the soul and causes the eventual destruction of the individual. Hoʻoponopono was and is essential to make things right. It was and is a process necessary to achieve lōkahi in life. Hoʻoponopono can only be achieved with aloha, haʻahaʻa (humility), mihi (forgiveness) and *hoʻihi* (respect) towards all three sides of the triangle.

    I could give a hundred examples of the wisdom and Aloha God has given to the Hawaiian people. However, my purpose is just to share a few examples so Christians can appreciate and find value in the Polynesian Culture.

TO THE PERSON OF HAWAIIAN ANCESTRY

By Pastor Steve Johnson

Please don't give up the True Good God that your ancestors knew. Don't give up the God who gave His only Son to bring you back to Himself, who prepared your people for the Good News, and whom your ancestors accepted with such joy. Please don't look at the human flaws of the good missionaries who gave their lives for you. All humans are far from perfect. Instead, see their Aloha and sacrifice for you. Don't blame them or your God for the false or fallen Christians who were not from your loving Father in Heaven. The Bible says, *"For such are false apostles, deceitful workers, transforming themselves into the Apostles of Christ. And no marvel; for Satan himself is transformed into an angel of light. Therefore it is no great thing if his ministers also be transformed as the ministers of righteousness; whose end shall be according to their works."* (2nd Corinthians 11:13-15) Don't be bitter, these people will be judged and punished for what they have done by your Father in Heaven. For the deeds they have done, and their false histories have not missed His all seeing eye.

As a Minister of Jesus Christ who is also a haole, I stand before you now representing all the Christians who have committed sins against you. I repent before you and I humbly ask for your forgiveness for the sins committed against you by my ancestors as well as by those today who call themselves Christians. My heart grieves over the many years of hurt and pain you have suffered unjustly at the hands of Christians. I know it is undeserved, but I humbly put myself at your mercy and ask for grace. I ask of you now, *"Please, forgive us!"*

TO MY PEOPLE

By Kahu John Kalili

The cry of many of today's Hawaiian leaders is to return to the old ways. The Hawaiians who want to return to the old religion should first consider the consequences of re-instituting the first kapu broken, that of free eating.

Women would not be allowed to eat together with the men on pain of immediate death. Women would no longer be able to eat ulua, kumu, bananas, coconut or pork without risking immediate death. No more banana cream pie, haupia, kulolo, laulau, kalua pig, or luau made with coconut milk for you ladies! If you Women's Libbers think that you are being discriminated against now, try returning to the kapu system!

Also, any of us Hawaiians not of pure ali'i blood, would no longer have any rights. An ali'i could come into our home and take anything he wanted from us, including one's wife or daughter. The only thing we would be able to do is lie flat on our face or die.

Don't forget that in the old religion the god Kū was a major god and any religion without his worship is definitely not Hawaiian. Common Hawaiians (Kanaka Maoli) were sacrificed to Kū regularly.

Going back to the old gods would bring back an oppression and cruelty far worse than the present situation. It is not only ridiculous but insane. Those who say that they are practicing the old religion are not telling the truth; they are creating a *new* religion of their own, aimed at achieving their own goals.

To return to a monarchy is also ridiculous. There is not one true surviving monarchy in the world today, because the system does not work. One King may be good, the next may be bad and cause the destruction of the kingdom. Such was the case of the Hawaiian Kingdom as bad ali'i squandered our land, natural resources and finances for their own selfish desires. Kalākaua was even warned by a prophet of God to change his ways or lose the kingdom. He refused.

Do you respect someone who blames all of his problems on others? A person who does this is not mature and loses the respect of his peers. To blame all of our woes on the haoles and other ethnic groups is also bad for our people because it implies that the Hawaiian people are helpless against them! It implies that others have total power over us. This is not true! However, when we make these "excuses" for our own failures to our children, it lowers their self esteem! Then they feel, *"Why fight it? Why try to better ourselves?"*

Many Hawaiians sit in despair and wait for Hawaiian Home lands as if it is their salvation, their only hope and way out. My people, only Iesū Kristo is our Savior, our only hope and way out! When we teach our children by our words and actions, *"Rip off the haoles, they ripped us off!"* we are telling them it is okay to be a criminal. There are more Hawaiian and part-Hawaiian children arrested than any other ethnic group, even though we are now only the fourth largest ethnic group in the islands! Not only that, it encourages our children to become the very thing we hated in others.

Because of this, many Hawaiians only "look like" Hawaiians. Spiritually and in their souls, the Hawaiian is dead. They have become all that was hated about the western culture. They only think about themselves and have no more Aloha in their hearts for anyone. The people who Robert Louis Stevenson called "*God's best and sweetest works*" are becoming extinct. Worse than dying as an ethnic group, we are dying spiritually as Hawaiians. Stevenson also said that his time among the Polynesians had "*bettered him greatly*". Would he say the same today?

The Hawaiian people are the people of Aloha. If we want to revive the true Hawaiian culture, we must first revive Aloha. Aloha is diametrically opposite to anger, bitterness, hatred and vengefulness. Therefore, to save our Hawaiian souls, these must be cast away. I know how difficult this is after all the hurts and injustices we have suffered, but for the sake of our people, our children and our islands, it must be done!

Our hurt runs so deep that only God can heal the hurt. Iesū knows our hurts because he went through hurts worse than ours. Only by giving them to Him and returning to our **TRUE** God can we be healed. Let us not be so proud as the ali'i of old, who would not submit to ho'oponopono, thus continuing bitterness and violence. Let us reconcile ourselves with our God and be healed of our hurts; then let us work towards bettering our peoples' situation in the spirit of Aloha.

It is God's will that we survive as a nation and a people. The Bible says in Revelation 7:9-10, "*After this I beheld, and, lo, a great multitude, which no man could number, of all nations, and kindreds, and people, and tongues, stood before the throne, and before the Lamb, clothed with white robes, and palms in their hands; And cried with a loud voice, saying, Salvation to our God which sitteth upon the throne, and unto the Lamb."* Read through the entire Bible. You will see that whenever a people and their leaders returned to God, He not only returned their sovereignty but richly blessed them.

As individuals, with or without sovereignty, we will be blessed, **IF** we do as the Bible commands. *"But seek ye first the kingdom of God and His righteousness; and all these things shall be added unto you."* (Matthew 6:33)

Sovereignty without God is vain, *"for what is a man profited, if he shall gain the whole world, and lose his own soul?"* (Matthew 16:26)

Seek God first, my people, and **HE** will take care of the rest. Matthew 11:28-29 says, *"Come unto me, all ye that labor and are heavy laden, and I will give you rest. Take my yoke upon you, and learn of me; for I am meek and lowly in heart: and ye shall find rest unto your souls."* Don't give up hope my people. For we can find righteousness, hope, peace and rest for our souls in Iesū Kristo. Amene

TO ALL

By Daniel Kikawa

Hoʻoponopono has begun. *Pule*, prayer has been offered to the One True God. The *hala*, transgression, has been stated and the *hihia*, negative entanglements, have been revealed.

Mihi, the confession of the wrongdoing, the asking for forgiveness, and the forgiving of the wrongdoing, are up to you. Without it, lōkahi (balance, peace, harmony) cannot be achieved and our ʻaina (land) will die; for *"the life of the land is perpetuated in righteousness."*

BOTH the asking of forgiveness and the forgiving must be done for the *kala*, loosening of the negative entanglements, to happen, and the curse over the land, *oki*, to be cut off.

Aloha ʻĀina . . . let us repent and forgive for the love of this land and for our children. *I hoʻokahi ka umauma, hoʻkahi ke aloha* . . . let us move forward, all abreast together, united in harmony and love. *Ua mau ke ea o ka ʻāina i ka pono, "The life of the land is perpetuated in righteousness."* This legacy first given to King Liholiho by his mother, the High Alii Keʻopuolani, on her death bed, has been cut short.

Her full legacy clearly shows what she really meant. She really was saying, *"The life of the land is perpetuated by the righteousness of Jesus Christ."*

Amen

END NOTES

1. Halley, *Halley's Bible Handbook*, p. 24

2. Padinjarekara, *Christ in the Ancient Vedas*

3. Pettazzoni, *The All-Knowing God*, p. 78

4. Metraux, *History of the Incas*, p. 125

5. Nelson, Genesis and the Mystery, pp. 12-16, 35

6. Harris, et al., *Theological Wordbook, vol. I*, p. 211

7. Gribetz, *The Timetables of Jewish History*, p. 8

8. Harris, et al., *Theological Wordbook, vol. I*, p. 42

9. De Vaux, *The Early History of Israel*, p. 281

10. Interviews with Malia Craver and Don Richardson

11. Kennedy, *The Real Meaning of the Zodiac*, p. 15
    Shore, ed., *Cassell's Biographical Dictionary*, p. 114

12. *Encyclopeadia Brittanica, vol. 1*, p. 518

13. Richardson, *Eternity in Their Hearts*, pp. 62-71

14. Richardson, *Eternity in Their Hearts*, pp. 133-141
    Halley, Halley's Bible Handbook, p. 24

15. Beckwith, *The Kumulipo*, p. 12

16. Allen, *The Betrayal of Liliuokalani*, pp. 117-118

17. For., *Acct. Poly. Race*, vol. 1, p. 60

18. Best, *The Maori As He Was*, p. 86

19. For., *Acct. Poly. Race, vol. 1*, p. 218

20. Pukui, *Hawaiian Dictionary*

21. Handy, *Ancient Hawn Civilization*, pp. 117-118
    Best, *Maori Religion and Mythology*, p. 94
    Taylor, *Paradise of the Pacific*, Dec. 1931, p. 78
    For., *Acct. Poly. Race, vol. 1*, p. 61

22. Pukui/Elbert, *Hawaiian Dictionary*, p. XII

23. Whatahoro, *The Lore of the Whare-Wananga*, p. 113

24. For., *Acct. Poly. Race, vol. 1*, p. 62

25. Whatahoro, *The Lore of the Whare-Wananga*, p. 113

26. Fornander, *Acct. Poly. Race, vol. 1*, p. 60

27. Pukui, *Nānā I Ke Kumu*, p. 122

28. Beckwith, *Hawaiian Mythology*, p. 370

29. Best, *Maori Religion and Mythology*, p. 94
    Whatahoro, *The Lore of the Whare-Wananga*, p. 106

30. Handy, *Polynesian Religion*, Bulletin 34, p. 96

31. Best, *Maori Religion and Mythology*, p. 90

32. Taylor, *Paradise of the Pacific*, Dec. 1931, p. 78

33. ibid.

34. Handy, *The Hawaiian Cult of 'Io*, p. 146-147

35. ibid.

36. *'Iolani*, May 1993

37. Metraux, *The History of the Incas*, p. 126

38. Handy, *Ancient Hawaiian Civilization*, pp. 43-45

39. ibid

40. Nelson/Broadberry, *Genesis and the Mystery*, p. 20

41. For., *Acct. Poly. Race, vol. 1*, p. 212

42. Buck, *The Coming of the Maori*, pp. 443-444

43. ibid., p. 444

44. Buck, *Vikings*, p. 274

45. Ngata, *The 'Io Cult*, pp. 336-337

46. Best, *Maori Religion and Mythology*, p. 91

47. ibid., p. 91

48. ibid., pp. 91-92

49. Stimson, *Tuamotuan Religion*, p. 74-79

50. Renan, *The History of the People of Israel*, p. 70

51. Harris, et al., *Theological Wordbook, vol. 1*, p. 210

52. Schmidt, *The Origin and Growth of Religion*, p. 268

53. Harris, et al., *Theological Wordbook, vol. 1*, pp. 46-47

54. Schmidt, *The Origin and Growth of Religion*, p. 271

55. Fornander, *Acct. Poly. Race, vol. 1*, p. 68

56. Handy, *Ancient Haw'n Civil.*, p. 48

57. Handy, *Polynesian Religion*, p. 97

58. For., *Acct. Poly. Race, vol. 1*, p. 215

59. Oral Hist. to Tomas Watene Rosser

60. For., *Acct. Poly. Race, vol. 1*, pp. 70-71
    Beckwith, *Haw' Myth.*, pp. 42-46

61. Fasold, *The Ark of Noah*, p. 72

62. ibid. p. 241

63. Webber, *God Divided the Nations*, p. 4

64. Schmidt, *The Origin and Growth of Religion*, p. 273

65. For., *Acct. Poly. Race, vol. 1*, p. 62

66. Cleator, *Lost Languages*, p. 111

67. For., *Acct. Poly. Race, vol. 1*, pp. 62-63, 66
    Tregear, *Maori-Polynesian Comparative Dictionary*
    Milner, *Samoan Dictionary*

68. Tregear, *Maori-Polynesian Dictionary*

69. Kepelino, *Kepelino's Traditions of Hawaii*, p. 32

70. Gifford, *Tongan Myths and Tales*, p. 15

71. Halley, *Halley's Bible Handbook*, p. 23

72. For., *Acct. Poly. Race, vol. 1*, p. 77

73. White, *Ancient Hist. of the Maori, vol. 1*, p. 153

74. For., *Acct. Poly. Race, vol. 1*, p. 77

75. Bunker, *Soo Thah*, pp. 87-94

76. Schmidt, *The Origin and Growth of Religion*, p.271

77. Thrum, *Hawaiian Folk Tales*, p. 29

78. Pukui, *Hawaiian Dictionary*
    Milner, *Samoan Dictionary*
    Charles Saletunoa Scanlan

79. For., *Acct. Poly. Race, vol. 1*, pp. 79-83

80. ibid., p. 85

81. Buck, *The Coming of the Maori*, p. 460

82. Pei Te Hurinui, *King Potatau*, p. 278

83. For., *Acct. Poly. Race, vol. 1*, pp. 83-85
    Beckwith, *Haw'n Myth.*, pp. 42-46
    Kepelino, *Kepelino's Trad. of Hi.*, p. 48

84. Kepelino, *Kepelino's Trad. of Hi.*, p. 48

85. For., *Acct. Poly. Race, vol. 1*, p. 65

86. Padinjarekara, *Christ in Ancient Vedas*, p. 153

87. Schmidt, *The Origin and Growth of Religion*, pp. 275-276

88. Handy, *Polynesian Religion*, Bulletin 34 ,p. 324

89. Best, *Maori Religion and Mythology*, p. 92

90. Handy, *Polynesian Religion*, p. 97

91. For., *Acct. Poly. Race, vol. 1*, p. 84

92. ibid., pp. 214-217

93. Buck, *The Coming of the Maori*, p. 520

94. For., *Acct. Poly. Race ,vol. 1*, p. 82

95. Tylor, *Researches*, p. 186

96. Halley, *Halley's Bible Handbook*, pp. 23-39
    Richardson, *Eternity in Their Hearts*, pp. 9-109

97. For., *Acct. Poly. Race, vol. 1*, pp. 86-87
    Kepelino, *Kepelino's Trad. of Hi.*, p. 42

98. White, *The Ancient Hist. of the Maori, vol. 1*, p. 172

99. Kepelino/Beckwith, *Kepelino's Trad.. Hi.*, p. 34

100. For., *Acct. Poly. Race, vol. 1*, pp. 91, 225-235
     Beckwith, *Haw'n Myth.*, pp. 314-316

101. Fasold, *The Ark of Noah*, p. 293

102. Kepelino/Beckwith, *Kepelino's Trad.. of Hi.*, p. 40

103. Thrum, *Hawaiian Folk Tales*, pp. 20-21
    For., *Acct. Poly. Race, vol. 1*, p. 42

104. Pei Te Hurinui, *King Potatau*, p. 254-255

105. For., *Acct. Poly. Race, vol. 1*, p. 91

106. Kepelino/Beckwith, *Kepelino's Trad. of Hi.*, p. 38

107. Tregear, *Maori-Polynesian Dictionary*

108. For., *Acct. Poly. Race, vol. 1*, p. 97

109. For., *Acct. Poly. Race, vol. 1*, pp. 96-97

110. Halley, *Bible Handbook*, pp. 44-45

111. Kennedy, *The Real Meaning of the Zodiac*, p.11

112. Strong, *Strong's Concordance, Hebrew and Chaldee Dictionary*, p. 102

113. ibid., p. 64

114. Fleming, *God's Voice in the Stars*, p. 29

115. Johnson/Mahelona, *Nā Inoa Hōkū*, p. 25-34

116. ibid., p. 23

117. Fale, *Tongan Astronomy*, p. 56

118. Harris, et al., *Theological Wordbook, vol. 2*, pp. 657,665

119. Kennedy, *The Real Meaning of the Zodiac*, p. 21

120. Seiss, *The Gospel In The Stars*, p. 37

121. ibid., p. 38

122. Johnson/Mahelona, *Nā Inoa Hōkū*, p. 110

123. Padinjaredara, *Christ in Ancient Vedas*, p. 42

124. Handy, *The Hawaiian Cult of 'Io*, p. 148-149

125. Handy, *The Hawaiian Cult of 'Io*, p. 151

126. Johnson/Mahelona, *Nā Inoa Hōkū*, p. 15

127. ibid., p. 110

128. Pratt, *Samoan Dictionary*
    Charles Saletunoa Scanlan

129. Fleming, *God's Voice in the Stars*, p. 38

130. ibid., p. 35

131. ibid., p. 36-37

132. trans., Tomas Watene Rosser

133. De Vaux, *The Early History of Israel*,
     pp. 272, 282, 460

134. Fleming, *God's Voice*, pp. 108-109

135. Seiss, *The Gospel in the Stars*, p. 116

136. Fleming, *God's Voice*, p. 109

137. Milner, *Samoan Dictionary*
     Charles Saletunoa Scanlan

138. For., *Acct. Poly. Race, vol. I*, pp. 118-119
     Malo, *Haw'n Antiquities*, p.141

139. For., *Acct. Poly. Race, vol. I*, p. 119

140. Fleming, *God's Voice*, pp. 105-107

141. Pukui/Elbert, *Haw'n Dictionary*, p. 224

142. Pettazzoni, *The All-Knowing God*, p. 7

143. Orbell, *The Natural World of the Maori*, p. 71
     trans.,Tomas Watene Rosser

144. Johnson/Mahelona, *Nā Inoa Hōkū*, p. 137

145. Seiss, *The Gospel in the Stars*, p. 45

146. Ryan, *The New Dictionary of Modern Maori*
     Tregear, *Maori-Polynesian Dictionary*
     Tomas Watene Rosser

147. Tregear, *Maori-Polynesian Dictionary*
     Tomas Watene Rosser

148. Tomas Watene Rosser

149. Hostetter, *Star Trek to Hawai'i*, p. 120

150. Tregear, *Maori-Polynesian Dictionary*, p. 393

151. Charles Saletunoa Scanlan

152. For., *Acct. Poly. Race, vol. 1*, pp. 97-99
     Beckwith, *Myth.*, pp. 322-323

153. For., *Acct. Poly. Race, vol. 1*, pp. 55, 98-99
     Beckwith, *Myth.*, p. 322

154. Beckwith, *Myth.*, p. 322

155. Dougherty, *To Steal A Kingdom*, p. 15

156. For., *Acct. Poly. Race*, vol. 1, p. 55, vol. 2, p. 6

157. Buck, *The Coming of the Maori*, p. 37

158. Kane, *The Voyagers*, p. 59

159. ibid., pp. 68-71

160. Buck, *Vikings of the Pacific*, p. 257

161. For., *Acct. Poly. Race, vol. 1*, p. 55
    Beckwith, *Myth.*, pp. 324-325

162. Buck, *Vikings*, p. 259

163. De Vaux, *The Early History of Israel*, p. 461

164. For., *Acct. Poly. Race, vol 1.*, p. 44

165. For., *Acct. Poly. Race, vol. 1*, p. 56

166. Halley, *Bible Handbook*, pp. 50-52
    Milman, *The History of the Jews, vol. 1*
    p. 100

167. Fasold, *The Ark Of Noah*, pp. 16-17

168. For., *Acct. Poly. Race, vol. 3*, p. 132

169. ibid., *vol. 1*, p. 40

170. ibid., *vol. 1*, pp. 100-101

171. ibid., p. 99
    Kepelino, *Kepelino's Trad. of Hi.*, pp. 68-74

172. For., *Acct. Poly. Race, vol. 1*, p. 100

173. Thrum, *Hawaiian Folk Tales*, p. 25

174. ibid., pp. 25-26

175. Beckwith, *The Kumulipo*, p. 176

176. For., *Memoirs of Bishop Museum, vol. VI*, p. 269

177. Allen, *The Betrayal of Lili'uokalani*, pp. 117-118

178. Davis, *Abraham Fornander: A Biography*, p. xiv

179. For., *Acct. Poly. Race, vol. 1*, pp. 181-185

180. Beckwith, *The Kumulipo*, pp. 7-8

181. ibid., p. 181

182. Beckwith, *Myth.*, p. 311

183. Beckwith, *The Kumulipo*, p. 48

184. Beckwith, *Myth.*, p. 311

185. Beckwith, *The Kumulipo*, p. 48

186. ibid., pp. 176-177

187. Dept. of Anthro., *History of Honaunau*, p. 139

188. ibid., p. 147

189. For., *Acct. Poly. Race, vol. 1*, pp. 22-23

190. Hostetter, *Star Trek to Hawai'i*, pp. 129-136

191. Watahoro, *Memoirs, vol. III*, p. 110

192. ibid., p. 10

193. Fasold, *The Ark of Noah*, p. XIV

194. Buck, *Vikings of the Pacific*, p. 21
    Best, *The Maori As He Was*, pp. 16-17

195. Best, *The Maori As He Was*, p. 18

196. Watahoro, *Mem., vol. III*, p. 11

197. Best, *The Maori As He Was*, pp. 17-18

198. Buck, *The Coming of the Maori*, p. 36

199. *Compton's Encyclopedia vol. 11*, p. 76

200. Mcleod, *Australia and New Zealand*, p. 120

201. For., *Acct. Poly. Race, vol. 2*, p. 8

202. Best, *The Maori As He Was*, p. 19

203. Buck, *The Coming of the Maori*, p. 72
    For., *The Poly. Race*, vol. 1, p. 57

204. For., *Acct. Poly. Race, vol. 1*, p. 23

205. ibid., p. 132-133

206. Latham (trans.), *Marco Polo*, p. 349

207. For., *Acct. Poly. Race, vol. 1*, p. 160

208. For., *Acct. Poly. Race*, vol. I, p. 162

209. Buck, *Vikings*, p. 318

210. ibid., p. 314

211. Irwin, *The Prehistoric Exploration and Colonization of the Pacific*, p. 100

212. *Science*, vol. 262, Oct. 29, 1993

213. Heyerdahl, *Sea Routes to Polynesia*, pp. 75-91

214. ibid., pp. 7, 35

215. Richardson, *Eternity in Their Hearts*, pp. 124-126

216. Siers, *Tonga*, p. 5

217. Matsunaga, Hon. Advertiser, *A '95 Odyssey of Education*, Sun., 9/11/94, A-3

218. Buck, *Vikings*, p. 283
Buck, *The Coming of the Maori*, p.36

219. Ngata, *Journal of Poly. Society, vol. 58-59*, p. 339

220. Taylor, *Paradise of the Pacific*, Dec. 1931, p. 78

221. Beckwith, *Haw'n Myth.*, p. 241

222. Beckwith, *Haw'n Myth*, pp. 240-242

223. Buck, *The Coming of the Maori*, p. 15

224. ibid., pp. 7-8, 11

225. Whatahoro, *Memoirs*, vol. III, p. 8

226. Richardson, *Eternity in Their Hearts*, p. 28

227. Grove, ed., *Webster's Third New International Dictionary*, unabridged, p. 1233
Cleveland, ed., *Britannica Atlas*, p. 129

228. Latham, *Travels of Marco Polo*, pp. 58-60, 350

229. Whatahoro, *Memoirs*, vol. III, p.6

230. Renan, *History of the People of Israel*, p. 70

231. Harris, et al., *Theological Wordbook of the Old Testament*, pp. 210-211

232. Richardson, *Eternity in Their Hearts*, p. 77
Bunker, *Soo Thah*, pp. 51-52

233. Forn., *Acct. Poly. Race, vol. 1*, p. 57

234. De Vaux, *The Early History of Israel*, p. 339

235. ibid.

236. Harris, et al., *Theological Wordbook*, vol. 1, p. 267
    Strong, *Exhaustive Concordance of the Bible*,
    p. 37 (Hebrew and Chaldee Dictionary section)

237. Fasold, The Ark of Noah, p. 241

238. Harris, et al., *Theological Wordbook*, vol. 1, p. 211
    Renan, *History of the People of Israel, vol. 1*, p. 69

239. ibid., p. 70

240. Harris, et al., *Theological Wordbook, vol. I*,
    pp. 484-485, 491-492

241. ibid., pp. 483-484
    Strong, *Strong's Exhaustive Concordance*, p. 33

242. Pukui & Elbert, *Hawaiian Dictionary*, p. 62

243. ibid., pp. 33, 50, 67

244. Best, *Maori Religion and Mythology*, p. 100

245. Pukui & Elbert, *Hawaiian Dictionary*, p. 44

246. Best, *Maori Religion & Mythology*, p. 165

247. Pratt, *Samoan Dictionary*, pg. 81

248. Charles Saletunoa Scanlan
    Troy Gentles

249. Oral hist. Cleighton Kuʻualohaokalaniakea Eaton
    Oral hist. from Tomas Watene Rosser

250. Hostetter, *Star Trek to Hawaiʻi*, p. 162

251. For., *Acct. Poly. Race, vol. 1*, p. 209

252. Both Ahuena Taylor and Malia Craver
    are descended from the line of Paʻao

253. Mitchell, *From God to God*, pp. 3-4

254. Buck, *Vikings*, pp. 262-263

255. Clark/Hon. Advertiser, *Number's up for Heiau on
    Kilauea's Hit List*

256. For. *Acct. Poly. Race, vol. 1*, p. 129

257. Pukui, *Nānā*, p. 122
     For., *Acct. Poly. Race*, vol. 1, p. 163

258. ibid., *vol. 2*, p. 63

259. Krauss, *Hon. Advertiser*, Sun. Jan. 15, 1995, p. D2

260. Montgomery, *Christus Redemptus*, p. 94
     Malo, *Antiquities*, pp. 58, 60-61

261. Montgomery, *Christus*, p. 97
     Malo, *Antiquities*, pp. 56-57

262. Kamakau, *Ruling Chiefs of Hi.*, pp. 232, 236

263. Kamakau, *Ruling Chiefs*, p. 232
     Sterling/*Summers, Sites of O'ahu*, p. 291

264. Sterling/Summers, *Sites*, p. 292

265. McAllister, *Archaeology of O'ahu*, p. 81

266. ibid., p. 71

267. Montgomery, *Christus*, pp. 95, 97
     Kamakau, *Ruling Chiefs*, pp. 229-232
     Malo, *Antiquities*, p. 62, 64

268. Potter/Kasdon, *Hawai'i Our Island State*, p. 46

269. Taylor, *Kapi'olani: A Memorial*, pp. 15-16

270. Both Malia Craver's (descendants of Pa'ao) and
     Ahuena Taylor's (descendants of Pili) ancestors
     knew about 'Io.

271. Dougherty, *To Steal*, p. 48

272. Emerson, *Pioneer Days in Hi.*, p. 4

273. Piercy, *Hawai'i Truth Stranger Than Fiction*, p. 40

274. Malo, *Haw'n Antiquities*, p. 142

275. Loomis, *By Faith*, pp. 4-5

276. Piercy, *Hawai'i's Missionary Saga*, p. 19

277. Brewster, *Memoir of Ke'opuolani*, p. 17

278. R. Johnson, Opukaha'ia grave site
     dedication, 2/17/94

279. Dwight, *Memoirs of Henry Obookiah*, p. 16

280. ibid., p. 78

281. Daws, *Shoal of Time*, p. 61

282. Opukaha'ia's gravestone rubbing, Mokuaikaua Church

283. Malo, *Haw'n Antiquities*, p. 145

284. Piercy, *Hawaii Truth*, p. 115

285. Feher, *Hawaii: A Pictorial History*, p. 178

286. Hon. Star Bulletin, *All About Hawai'i*, pp. 28-29

287. Mitchell, *Hawaiian Culture*, p. 80

288. Loomis, *By Faith*, pp. 4-7

289. Gessler, *Hawai'i, Isles of Enchantment*, p. 58
    Kailua-Kona Walking Tour Map

290. Loomis, *By Faith*, pp. 4-7

291. Gessler, *Hawai'i, Isles of Enchantment*, p. 59
    Taylor, *Hon. Star Bulletin*, Mon., June 19, 1961

292. Oral history to Tomas Watene Rosser
    from Moape Bogiru of Bau, Viti Levu Fiji

293. Shortland, *Traditions and Superstitions
    of the New Zealanders*, p. 120

294. Padinjaredara, *Christ in Ancient Vedas*, p. 42

295. Handy, *The Hawaiian Cult of 'Io*, p. 151

296. Marocco, *Hawaii's Great Awakening*,
    pp. 21, 24, 32

297. Schmitt, *Hist. Stats*, p. 35

298. Kamakau, *Ruling Chiefs*, p. 259

299. Piercy, *Hawaii Truth*, p. 24

300. Brewster, *Memoir of Ke'opuolani*, p. 19

301. Allen, *The Betrayal of Lili'uokalani*, p. 151

302. Piercy, *Hawaii Truth*, p. 104

303. Kamakau, *Ruling Chiefs*, p. 384

304. ibid., pp. 352-356

305. Loomis, *By Faith*, pp. 4-7

306. Marocco, *Great Awakening*, p. 28

307. Loomis, *To All People*, p. 17

308. ibid., p. 32

309. ibid., p. 33

310. Daws, *Shoal of Time*, p. 92

311. The Constitution of 1840

312. The Constitution of 1852

313. Allen, *Betrayal of Lili.*, p. 301

314. Daws, *Shoal*, p. 127
    Loomis, *To All People*, p. 28

315. Loomis, *To All People*, pp. 27-28

316. Piercy, *Hawai'i Truth*, p. 21

317. Kamakau, *Ruling Chiefs*, p. 234

318. Wisniewski, *Rise and Fall*, p. 41

319. Loomis, *To All People*, pp. 10-11

320. ibid., p. 12

321. ibid., p. 41

322. Piercy, *Hawaii Truth*, p. 79

323. Schmitt, *Hist. Stats*, p. 229

324. Piercy, *Hawaii Truth*, p. 79

325. Wisniewski, *Rise and Fall*, p. 41

326. Allen, *Betrayal*, p. 301

327. ibid., p. 207

328. Dougherty, *To Steal*, pp. 81,103
    Piercy, *Hawaii Truth*, p. 14

329. Lili'uokalani, *Hawaii's Story*, p. 9

330. Daws, *Shoal*, p. 109

331. Loomis, *To All People*, pp. 24-25

332. Dougherty, *To Steal*, p. 109

333. Allen, *Betrayal*, p. 125

334. Daws, *Shoal*, pp. 184-185

335. Loomis, *To All People*, p. 34

336. Daws, *Shoal*, pp. 246-249

337. ibid., pp. 251-252

338. Daws, *Shoal*, p. 251

339. Daws, *Shoal*, p. 162

340. Oral history from Kahu John A. Kalili

341. Allen, *Betrayal*, p. 190

342. ibid., p. 343

343. The Native Hawaiian Land Trust Task Force, *The Prophetic Vision of Ke'opuolani, The Sacred Queen of Hawaii*

344. ibid.

345. Lili'uokalani, *Hawaii's Story*, p. xii

346. Roth, Ed., *The Price of Paradise*, pp. 195-203

347. Kam. School Report, July, 1983, p. 24

348. Piercy, *Hawaii Truth*, pp. 32-33

349. Daws, *Shoal*, pp. 101-102

350. Piercy, *Hawaii Truth*, p. 21

351. Allen, *Betrayal*, p. 125

352. Dougherty, *To Steal*, p. 170

353. Ambrose, Hon. Star Bulletin, *The Keaulana Ohana* Wed., 6/1/94, D-1

354. Shook, *Ho'oponopono*, p. 4

355. Ambrose, Hon. Star Bulletin, *The Keaulana Ohana* Wed., 6/1/94, D-5

356. Shook, *Ho'oponopono*, pp. 10-12

357. Pukui, *Nānā*, p. 247

358. Allen, *Betrayal*, p. 190

359. Shook, *Ho'oponopono*, pp. 10-12

360. Pukui, *Nānā*, p. 233

SUGGESTED READING

Allen, H. *The Betrayal of Lili'uokalani*. Glendale, Ca. : Mutual, 1982

Bullinger, E.W. *The Witness of the Stars*. Mich.: Kregel Publishing, 1967

Daws, G. *Shoal of Time*. Honolulu: University of Hawai'i Press, 1968

Dwight, E. *Memoirs of Henry Obookiah*. Ed. Wolfe, E. Honolulu: Woman's Board of Missions for the Pacific Islands, 1990

Fleming, K. *God's Voice in the Stars*. New Jersey: Loizeaux Bro., 1981

Halley, H. *Halley's Bible Handbook*. Minnesota: Zondervan, 1962

Kang, C.H. & Nelson, E. *The Discovery of Genesis*. St. Louis, Mo.: Concordia Publishing House, 1979

Kennedy, J. *The Real Meaning of the Zodiac*. Florida: Coral Ridge Ministries, 1989

Loomis, A. *By Faith*. Honolulu: Offset Printing House, 1980

Marocco, J. *Hawaii's Great Awakening*. Bartimaeus Publishing. Kahului, Hi. , 1991

McDowell, J. *Evidence That Demands A Verdict, vol. 1 & 2*. CA: Here's Life Publishers, 1972

Morris, H. *The Genesis Record*. Grand Rapids, MI.: Baker Book House, 1976

-------. *Scientific Creationism*. CA: Master Books, 1974

The Native Hawaiian Land Trust Task Force. *The Prophetic Vision of Ke'opuolani, The Sacred Queen of Hawai'i*. Hawai'i: Hawaiian Almanac Publishing, 1982

Richards, W. *Memoir of Ke'opuolani*. Boston: Crocker & Brewster, 1825

Richardson, D. *Eternity in Their Hearts*. Ventura, CA: Regal, 1981

Seiss, J. *The Gospel in the Stars*. 1882; rpt. Grand Rapids, Michigan: Kregel, 1972

Shook, E. *Ho'oponopono*. Honolulu: The East-West Center, 1985

Taylor, P. *Kapi'olani: A Memorial*. Honolulu: Grieve, 1897

BIBLIOGRAPHY

Allen, H. *The Betrayal of Lili'uokalani.* Glendale, Ca. : Mutual, 1982

Alpers, A. *The World of the Polynesians.* 1970; rpt. Auckland, N.Z.: Oxford University Press, 1987

Ambrose, G. "The Keaulanan Ohana." *Honolulu Star-Bulletin.* June 1, 1994

Baron, S. *A Social and Religious History of the Jews, vol. 1.* N.Y.: Columbia Univesity Press, 1958

Barre're, D. *The Kumuhonua Legends.* Honolulu: Bishop Museum, 1969

Beckwith, M. *Hawaiian Mythology.* 1940; rpt. Honolulu: University of Hawai'i Press, 1970

-----. ed. *Kumulipo.* 1951; rpt. Honolulu: University Press of Hawai'i

Best, E. *The Maori As He Was.* Wellington, N.Z.: A.R. Shearer, Government Printer, 1974

-----. *Maori Religion and Mythology.* No. 10-11. *Dominion Museum Bulletin.* Wellington, N.Z.: W.A.G. Skinner, Government Printer,1924

-----. *The Astronomical Knowledge of the Maori.* No. 3. *Dominion Museum Bulletin.* Wellington, N. Z.: W.A.G. Skinner, Government Printer, 1922

-----. *The Maori Canoe.* No. 7. *Dominion Museum Bulletin.* Wellington, N.Z.: A.R. Shearer, Government Printer, 1925

Bingham, H. *A Residence of Twenty-One Years in the Sandwich Islands.* Hartford: Hezekiah Huntington, 1847

Brandewie, E. *Wilhelm Schmidt and the Origin of the Idea of God.* Lanham, M.D.: University Press of America, 1983

Bryan, E., Emory, K., et al. *The Natural and Cultural History of Honaunau, Kona, Hawai'i.* Honolulu: Bernice Pauahi Bishop Museum, 1986

Buck, P. *The Coming of the Maori*. Christchurch, N.Z.: Whitcombe & Tombs Ltd., 1949

-------. *Vikings of the Pacific*. Chicago: University of Chicago Press, 1959

Bullinger, E.W. *The Witness of the Stars*. Mich.: Kregel Publishing, 1967

Bunker, A. *Soo Thah. A Tale of the Making of the Karen Nation*. New York: Fleming H. Revell Co., 1902

Clark. "Number's Up for Heiau on Kīlauea's Hit List." *Honolulu Advertiser*. Newspaper. Honolulu

Cleator, P. *Lost Languages*. London: The Camelot Press, 1959

Cleveland, W. ed. *Britannica Atlas*. Chicago: Encyclopaedia Britannica, 1991

Coan, T. *Life In Hawai'i*. N.Y.: Anson D.F. Randolph & Co.,1882

Curtis C. *Builders of Hawai'i*. Honolulu: Kamehameha Schools, 1966

Davis, C. *The Life And Times Of Patuone*. Auckland, N.Z.: Steam Printing Co., 1876

Davis, E. *Abraham Fornander: A Biography*. Honolulu: University Press of Hi., 1979

Daws, G. *Shoal of Time*. Honolulu: University of Hawai'i Press, 1968

De Vaux, R. *The Early History of Israel*. Trans. Smith, D. Philadelphia: The Westminster Press, 1978

Dixon, R.B. *The Mythology of All Races*. vol. IX of *Oceania*. Cambridge, Mass.: University Press, 1916

Dougherty, M. *To Steal A Kingdom*. Waimanalo, Hi. : Island Style Press, 1992

Dudley, M. *Man, Gods, and Nature*. Honolulu: Na Kāne O Ka Malo Press, 1990

Dwight, E. *Memoirs of Henry Obookiah*. Ed. Wolfe, E. Honolulu: Woman's Board of Missions for the Pacific Islands, 1990

Emerson, O.P. *Pioneer Days in Hawaii*. New York: Doubleday, Doran & Co., 1928

Erickson, J. ed. *Sunset South Pacific Travel Guide*. Menlo Park, CA: Lane Publishing, 1980

Fale, T. *Tongan Astronomy*. Tonga: Polynesian Eyes Foundation, 1990

Fasold, D. *The Ark Of Noah*. New York: Wynwood Press, 1988

Feher, J. *Hawaii: A Pictorial History*. Honolulu: Bishop Museum, 1969

Fischman, J. "Going for the Old: Ancient DNA Draws a Crowd." *Science*. vol. 262. Oct. 29, 1993

Fleming, K. *God's Voice in the Stars*. New Jersey: Loizeaux Bro., 1981

Fornander, A. *An Account of the Polynesian Race*. 3 vols. London, 1878-1885; rpt. Rutland, Vt. : Charles E. Tuttle Co., 1969

-------. *Fornander Collection of Hawaiian Antiquities and Folk-lore*. vol. IV of the *Memoirs of the Bernice Pauahi Bishop Museum*. ed. Thrum, T. Honolulu: Bishop Museum, 1916-1917

-------. Fornander Collection of Hawaiian Antiquities and Folk-lore. vol. V of the *Memoirs of the Bernice Pauahi Bishop Museum*. ed. Thrum,T. Honolulu: Bishop Museum, 1918-1919

-------. *Fornander Collection of Hawaiian Antiquities and Folk-lore*. vol. VI of the *Memoirs of the Bernice Pauahi Bishop Museum*. Honolulu: Bishop Museum, 1919-1920

Gessler, C. *Hawai'i, Isles of Enchantment*. N.Y.: D. Appleton-Century, 1937

Gifford, E. *Tongan Myths & Tales*. bul. 8. *Bernice P. Bishop Museum*. Honolulu: The Bishop Museum, 1924

Gish, D. *Evolution, the Fossils Say No!*. Creation-Life Publishers, 1979

Gove, P. ed. *Webster's Third New International Dictionary of the English Language, Unabridged*. Springfield, Mass.: G. & C. Merriam Co., 1971

Gowen, H. *The Napoleon of the Pacific*. New York: Fleming H. Revell Co., 1919

Gribetz, J. *The Timetables of Jewish History*. N.Y.: Simon & Schuster, 1993

Halley, H. *Halley's Bible Handbook*. Minnesota: Zondervan, 1962

Handy, E.S.C. *Polynesian Religion*. bul. 34. *Bishop Museum*. Honolulu: Bishop Museum,1927

-------. "Religion and Education." in *Ancient Hawaiian Civilization, A Series of Lectures*. Ed. Pratt, H. Honolulu: Kamehameha Schools, 1933

-------. *The Hawaiian Cult of 'Io.* vol. 50-51 *Journal of the Polynesian Society.* Wellington: The Polynesian Society, 1941

Handy, E.S.C. and Pukui, M.K. *The Polynesian Family System in Ka'ū, Hawai'i.* Wellington, N.Z.: Polynesian Society, 1958

Hawai'i Criminal Justice Data Center. *Crime in Hawai'i, 1989.* Honolulu: Hawai'i Judiciary, 1990

Hawai'i Dept. of Planning & Research. *Historical Statistics of Hawai'i, 1778-1962.* Honolulu: Dept. of Planning & Research, 1962

Harris, R.; Archer, G. & Waltke, B. *Theological Wordbook of the Old Testament.* vol 1-2. Chicago: Moody Press

Heyerdahl, T. *Sea Routes to Polynesia.* Chicago: Rand McNally, 1968

Hostetter, C. *Star Trek to Hawai'i.* San Luis Obispo, CA: The Diamond Press, 1991

Honolulu Star Bulletin. *All About Hawai'i.* Honolulu: Honolulu Star Bulletin, Feb. 1936

'I'ī, J. *Fragments of Hawaiian History.* Trans. Pukui, M. Honolulu: Bishop Museum Press, 1959

Irwin, G. *The Prehistoric Exploration and Colonisation of the Pacific.* Cambridge, U.K.: Cambridge University Press, 1992

Johnson, R. & Mahelona J. *Na Inoa Hōkū.* Honolulu: Topgallant, 1975

Kamakau, S. *Ruling Chiefs of Hawai'i.* Trans. Pukui, M., et al. Honolulu: Kamehameha School Press, 1961

Kamakau, S. *Tales and Traditions of the People of Old.* Trans. Pukui, M. Ed. Barre're, D. Honolulu: Bishop Museum Press, 1991

Kamehameha Schools/Bernice Pauahi Bishop Estate. *Native Hawaiian Educational Assessment Project.* Final Report. July, 1983

Kanahele, G. *Current Facts and Figures About Hawaiians.* Honolulu: Project Waiaha, 1982

Kanahele, G. *Kū Kanaka.* Honolulu: University of Hawai'i Press, 1986

Kane, H. *The Voyagers.* Bellevue, WA.: WhaleSong, 1991

Kang, C.H. & Nelson, E. *The Discovery of Genesis.* St. Louis, Mo: Concordia Publishing House, 1979

Kennedy, J. *The Real Meaning of the Zodiac*. Florida: Coral Ridge Ministries, 1989

Kepelino. *Kepelino's Traditions of Hawaii*. Bulletin 95. *Bernice P. Bishop Museum*. Ed. Beckwith, M. 1932; rpt. Millwood, N.Y.: Kraus Reprint Co., 1978

-----. Kepelino's *"Hawaiian Collection": His "Hooiliili Havaii,"* Pepa I. vol. 11. *The Hawaiian Journal of History*. Trans. Kirtley, B. & Mookini, E. Ed. Jackson, F. 1858; rpt. Honolulu: Hawaiian Historical Society, 1977

Kuykendall, R.S. *The Hawaiian Kingdom*. vol. II. Honolulu: University of Hawai'i Press, 1953

Kuykendall, R.S. *The Hawaiian Kingdom*. vol. III. Honolulu: University of Hawai'i Press, 1967

Lang, A. *The Making of Religion*. London: Longmans, Green & Co., 1898

Langdon, R. *The Lost Caravel Re-Explored*. Australia: Brolga Press, 1988

Latham, R. trans. *The Travels of Marco Polo*. London: Penguin, 1958

Lili'uokalani, L. *Hawai'i's Story by Hawai'i's Queen*. Honolulu: Mutual Publishing, 1990

Loomis, A. *By Faith*. Honolulu: Offset Printing House, 1980

Loomis, A. *To All People*. Tennessee: Hawai'i Conference of the United Church of Christ, 1970

Malo, D. *Hawaiian Antiquities*. Trans. Emerson, N. Honolulu: Bishop Museum Press, 1951

Marocco, J. *Hawaii's Great Awakening*. Bartimaeus Publishing. Kahului, Hi. , 1991

Matsunaga, M. "A '95 Odyssey of Education." *The Honolulu Advertiser*. Sept. 11, 1994

McAllister, J.G. *Archaeology of O'ahu*. Bulletin 104. *Bernice P. Bishop Museum*. 1933; rpt. Millwood, N.Y.: Kraus Reprint Co., 1971

McDowell, J. *Evidence That Demands A Verdict, vol. 1 &2*. CA: Here's Life Publishers, 1972

McHenry, R. ed. *Encyclopaedia Britannica, vol. 1*. Chicago: Encyclopaedia Brittanica, 1993

McLean, G.S., Oakland, R. and McLean, L. *The Evidence for Creation*. Eston, Canada: Full Gospel Bible Institute, 1989

Mead, S. et. al. *Te Maori*. New York: Harry N. Abrams, 1984

Metraux, A. *The History of the Incas*. New York: Random House, 1969

Milman, H. *The History of the Jews, vol. 1*. London: J.M. Dent & Sons, 1909

Milner, G.B. *Samoan Dictionary*. 1966. rpt. Samoa: Gov't. of American Samoa, 1979

Mitchell, D. *Resource Units in Hawaiian Culture*. Honolulu: The Kamehameha Schools Press, 1982

Mitchell, R. *From God to God*. Oahu: 1979

Montgomery, H. *Christus Redemptor*. MacMillan, 1906

Morris, H. *The Genesis Record*. Grand Rapids, MI.: Baker Book House, 1976

-------. *Scientific Creationism*. CA: Master Books, 1974

Mulholland. *Hawaii's Religions*. Rutland, Vt. : C.E. Tuttle Co., 1970

The Native Hawaiian Land Trust Task Force. *The Prophetic Vision of Ke'opuolani, The Sacred Queen of Hawai'i*. Hawai'i: Hawaiian Almanac Publishing, 1982

Nelson, E. *Genesis and the Mystery Confucius Couldn't Solve*. St. Louis, MO.:Concordia Publishing House, 1994

Orbell, M. *The Natural World of the Maori*. Dobbs Ferry, N.Y.: Sheridan House, 1985

Padinjarekara, J. *Christ in Ancient Vedas*. Burlington, ON.: Welch Publishing Co., 1991

Pei Te Hurinui. *King Potatau*. Wellington N.Z.: The Polynesian Society, 1959

Pettazzoni, R. *The All Knowing God; Researches into Early Religion and Culture*. London: Methuen, 1956

Piercy, L. *Hawaii Truth Stranger Than Fiction*. Honolulu: Fisher, 1985

------. *Hawai'i's Missionary Saga*. Honolulu: Mutual Publishing, 1992

Potter, N. & Kasdon, L. *Hawai'i Our Island State*. Ohio: Charles E. Merrill Books, 1964

Pratt, G. *Samoan Dictionary*. Samoa: London Missionary Society Press, 1862

Pukui, M. & Elbert, S. *Hawaiian-English Dictionary*. Honolulu: University of Hawai'i Press, 1957

Pukui, M., Haertig, E.W., Lee, C. *Nānā I Ke Kumu*. 2 vols. Honolulu: Hui Hanai, 1972

Renan, R. *History of the People of Israel*. vol. 1. Boston: Roberts Bros., 1896

Richards, W. *Memoir of Ke'opuolani*. Boston: Crocker & Brewster, 1825

Richardson, D. *Eternity in Their Hearts*. Ventura, CA: Regal, 1981

Roth, R., Ed. *The Price of Paradise*. Honolulu: Mutual, 1992

Rose, R. *Hawai'i: The Royal Isles*. Honolulu: Bishop Museum, 1980

Ryan, P.M. *The New Dictionary of Modern Maori*. Auckland, N.Z.: Heinemann, 1974

Schmitt, R. *Historical Statistics of Hawai'i*. Honolulu: University of Hawai'i Press, 1977

------. *The Missionary Censuses of Hawai'i*. Honolulu: Bishop Museum, 1973

Schmidt, W. *The Origin and Growth of Religion*. Trans. Rose, H. J. London: Methuen & Co., 1935

Seiss, J. *The Gospel in the Stars*. 1882; rpt. Grand Rapids, MI.: Kregel, 1972

Shore, T. ed. *Cassell's Biographical Dictionary*. London: Cassell, Petter, and Galpin, 1867

Shook, E. *Ho'oponopono*. Honolulu: The East-West Center, 1985

Shortland, E. *Traditions and Superstitions of the New Zealanders*. 1856; rpt. New York: AMS Press, 1980

Siers, J. *Tonga*. Wellington, N.Z.: Millwood Press, 1978

Sinclair, K. ed. *The Oxford Illustrated History of New Zealand*. Auckland, N.Z.: Oxford University Press

Silverman, J. *Ka'ahumanu, Molder of Change*. Honolulu: Friends of the Judiciary History Cntr. of Hawai'i, 1987

Smith, P. *Journal of the Polynesian Society.* supplement. vol. 29-30.
  Wellington, N.Z.: The Polynesian Society, 1920

State of Hawai'i. *Hawai'i Basic Data and Information Book on
  Hawaiians.* Honolulu: The Office, 1983

Sterling, E. & Summers, C. Editors. *Sites of O'ahu.* Honolulu: Bishop
  Museum, 1978

Stimson, J.F. *The Cult of Kiho-tuma.* Bulletin 111. *Bernice P.
  Bishop Museum.* Honolulu: The Museum, 1933

Strong, J. *Abingdon's Strong's Exhaustive Concordance of the Bible.* 1890;
  rpt. Nashville: Abingdon, 1890

Taylor, C. "Tales About Hawai'i." *Honolulu Star Bulletin.* Newspaper.
  Honolulu: Monday, June 19, 1961

Taylor, E.A. "The Cult of 'Iolani." *Paradise of the Pacific.* Dec. 1931

Taylor, P. *Kapi'olani: A Memorial.* Honolulu: Grieve, 1897

Tenney, M. ed. *Pictorial Encyclopedia of the Bible.* vol. 1-4. Grand Rapids,
  Michigan: Zondervan, 1975

Te Haupapa-o-tane. *'Io, The Supreme God, and Other Gods Of The Maori.*
  vol. 29-30. *Journal of the Polynesian Society.* Wellington, N.Z.:
  The Polynesian Society, 1920

Tregear, E. *Maori-Polynesian Comparative Dictionary.* Wellington, N.Z.:
  Lyon & Blair, 1891

Thrum, T. *Hawaiian Folk Tales.* Chicago: A.C. McClurg & Co., 1912

Tylor, E. *Researches Into the Early History of Mankind
  and the Development of Civilization.* 1865;
  rpt. Chicago: University of Chicago Press, 1964

University of Chicago, ed. *Compton's Encyclopedia.* U.S.A.: Compton
  Co., 1985

Webber, D., et al. *God Divided the Nations.* Oklahoma City, OK:
  The Southwest Radio Church, 1981

Whatahoro, H.T. *The Lore of the Whare-Wananga.* pt. 1. vol. 3-4. *Memoirs
  of the Polynesian Society.* Trans. Smith, P. New Plymoth, N.Z.:
  Thomas Avery, 1913

Whiston, W. trans. *The Works of Josephus.* Peabody, Mass.: Hendrickson
  Publishers, 1985

White, J. *The Ancient History of the Maori, His Mythology and Traditions.* vols. 1 & 2. Wellington: George Didsbury, Government Printer, 1887

Wilkinson, R. *A Malay - English Dictionary.* London: MacMillan, 1959

Wisniewski, R. *The Rise and Fall of the Hawaiian Kingdom.* Honolulu: Pacific Basin Ent., 1979

ALOHA KE AKUA'S POSITION ON SOVEREIGNTY

God is Sovereign

Matthew 16:26 "For what is a man profited if he shall gain the whole world, and lose his own soul?"

What good is "sovereignty" if Hawaiian souls are lost for eternity?

Matthew 6:33 "But seek ye first the kingdom of God, and his righteousness; and all these things shall be added unto you."

When the leaders of any people and the people themselves seek God first and His righteousness, God has ALWAYS restored their sovereignty. More than this, He provides protection and blesses that nation abundantly.

ALOHA KE AKUA

Aloha Ke Akua (God is Love) is an interdenominational Christian ministry.

The purpose of this ministry is ho'oponopono, in order to heal the land.

If you are interested in receiving more information about Aloha Ke Akua, ordering books and other material, sponsoring or attending an Aloha Ke Akua presentation, or making a financial contribution to Aloha Ke Akua, please contact:

Aloha Ke Akua
HCR2 Box 6640
Kea'au, Hawai'i 96749
Ph. (808) 948-3474